Church on Earth

Other books in the Lutheran Voices series

Given for You
by Louis W. Accola

Faith's Wisdom for Daily Living
by Herbert Anderson and Bonnie Miller-McLemore

Getting Ready for the New Life
by Richard F. Bansemer

Listen! God Is Calling!
by D. Michael Bennethum

God in the Raging Waters
by Paul Blom

On Earth as in Heaven
by Kay Bender Braun

The Letter and the Spirit
by David Brondos

Leading on Purpose
by Eric Burtness

A Life Worth Leading
by Eric Burtness

Open the Doors and See All the People
by Norma Cook Everist

Connecting with God in a Disconnected World
by Carolyn Coon Mowchan and Damian Anthony Vraniak

Holy Purpose
by Carolyn Coon Mowchan

On a Wing and a Prayer
by Michael L. Cooper-White

Living Lutheran
by Dave Daubert

Let the Servant Church Arise!
by Barbara DeGrote-Sorensen and David Allen Sorensen

People of Purpose
by Robert Driver-Bishop

Our Lives Are Not Our Own
by Harold Eppley and Rochelle Melander

Emerging Ministry
by Nathan C. P. Frambach

Reclaiming the "C" Word
by Kelly A. Fryer

Reclaiming the "E" Word
by Kelly A. Fryer

Reclaiming the "L" Word
by Kelly A. Fryer and Timothy F. Lull

Water from the Rock
by Ann E. Hafften

Who Do You Say That I Am?
by Susan K. Hedahl and Adele Stiles Resmer

Signs of Belonging
by Mary E. Hinkle

Sanctified Living
by Frank Honeycutt

Called by God to Serve
by Robert F. Holley and Paul E. Walters

On Being Lutheran
by Timothy F. Lull

Ending Poverty
by Nancy E. Maeker and Peter Rogness

Speaking of Trust
by Martin E. Marty

Will I Sing Again?
by John McCullough Bade and Cynthia Prestholdt

Public Church
by Cynthia D. Moe-Lobeda

Give Us This Day
by Craig L. Nessan and David Beckmann

Living in the Kingdom
by Alvin N. Rogness and Peter Rogness

The Word of the Cross in a World of Glory
by Philip Ruge-Jones

Praying for Reform
by William R. Russell

Lutheran Identity
by Frank C. Senn

War, Peace, and God
by Gary M. Simpson

Gravity and Grace
by Joseph Sittler and Martin E. Marty

Blessed to Follow
by Martha E. Stortz

American Destiny and the Calling of the Church
by Paul A. Wee

Church on Earth

Grounding Your Ministry in a Sense of Place

Jeff Wild and Peter Bakken

Augsburg Fortress
Minneapolis

CHURCH ON EARTH
Grounding Your Ministry in a Sense of Place

Purchases of multiple copies of this book are available at a discount from the publisher. For more information, contact the sales department at Augsburg Fortress, Publishers, 1-800-328-4648, or write to: Sales Director, Augsburg Fortress, Publishers, Box 1209, Minneapolis, MN 55440-1209.

Materials for a single- or multiple-session study of *Church on Earth* are downloadable free of charge at www.augsburgfortress.org

Library of Congress Cataloging-in-Publication Data
Wild, Jeff, 1954-
Church on earth : grounding your ministry in a sense of place / Jeff Wild and Peter Bakken.
p. cm.— (Lutheran voices)
Includes bibliographical references (p.).
ISBN 978-0-8066-8012-5 (alk. paper)
1. Pastoral theology—Lutheran Church. 2. Parishes. 3. Religion and geography. 4. Madison Christian Community (Madison, Wis.) I. Bakken, Peter W., 1957- II. Title.

BX8071.W56 2009
253—dc22 2008047420

The paper used in this publication meets the minimum requirements of American National Standard for Information Sciences—Permanence of Paper for Printed Library Materials, ANSI Z329.48-1984.

Manufactured in the U.S.A.

From Jeff to Nan—
From Peter to Martha and Mara—
Thanks for your gift of space to work on this project
and your patient support throughout.

Contents

Prologue

> What other church is there besides institutional? Friedrich von Hugel said the institution of the church is like the bark on the tree. There's no life in the bark. It's dead wood. But it protects the life of the tree within. And the tree grows and grows and grows and grows. If you take the bark off, it's prone to disease, dehydration, death. So yes, the church is dead but it protects something alive. And when you have a church without bark, it doesn't last long. It disappears, gets sick and it's prone to all kinds of disease, heresy, and narcissism.
>
> —Eugene Peterson

So said Peterson, the renowned author and pastor, in response to an interviewer's question about the institutional church. We agree with Peterson and von Hugel: the institutional church is indeed like the bark on a tree, a treasure in an earthen vessel. We, too, are concerned about congregations that decline in members in spite of their best efforts, and the gradual erosion of the church's place in North America. We contend, however, that if congregations are focusing solely on ways to maintain or flourish as an institution, they are barking up the wrong tree.

Church on Earth is an effort to examine the tree's roots and calls for an analysis of the soil that anchors the tree in its place. Just as nutrients in the soil feed a tree's roots and those roots hold the soil in place, there is a symbiotic relationship between a congregation and the place where it is located. Every congregation, though similar to other trees in the woods, has a unique identity shaped in part by its understanding of and relationship to the place where it is planted to carry forth its mission. We have written this book because we believe that attending to place as a dimension of human experience can provide a new perspective on the mission, ministry, and proclamation of the local congregation, providing more concrete ways of relating Christian theology of creation and redemption to people's lives and engaging the church more constructively with contemporary needs and possibilities in God's world.

This book is a modest contribution to the discussion about the life and mission of a congregation as it seeks to live out its mission faithfully. It is modest primarily because the congregations we belong to are not in the same place as your congregation, which limits our ability to talk in specifics. Nevertheless, we assume that we share things in common: a Lutheran theological perspective, attentiveness to Scripture, a love for Christ and his church, gratitude for creation, and a willingness to live out our vocation as stewards where we are placed. This book is modest also because we are more interested in growing deeper in relationship to God and with creation—including both human and nonhuman life—than in growing bigger, rounder, and taller than all the other trees in the forest. If you share this desire we hope this book will deepen the congregation where you are rooted and help it to grow and bear good fruit.

Church on Earth is a biblical and theological reflection contextualized in a place called Madison Christian Community (MCC). Located on the west side of Madison, Wisconsin, MCC is a shared ecumenical ministry founded in the 1960s when such endeavors were first being undertaken in earnest by mainline denominations. 2008 was the fortieth anniversary of two congregations from two such denominations—Community of Hope (United Church of Christ) and Advent Lutheran (ELCA)—joining together to live out this ecumenical vision that is now MCC. Jeff Wild, an ELCA pastor, serves as one of the pastors at MCC. Peter Bakken, coordinator for Public Policy at the Wisconsin Council of Churches, is also a member of Advent and MCC. Where we share personal stories in this volume, we refer to ourselves in the third person.

This volume reflects on every page our deep appreciation for the vision, values, and dedicated work of MCC members, staff, and congregational leadership over the past four decades. They have made MCC a vital and creative community of faith, an outstanding example of a church that embodies a sense of place in the way it cherishes its land, serves its community, and works for peace and justice throughout the world.

We are grateful also to James Bailey, director of the Lay School of Theology in the South Central Synod of Wisconsin, ELCA, and retired professor of Wartburg Seminary, for his invitation to present this material for a class in spring 2008. The questions, feedback, and encouragement we received from the participants in this course were a great help in the formation of this book. Thank you.

1

Called to Cultivate and Care for Our Places

No matter where you go, there you are.

—Yogi Berra

Yogi Berra's famous aphorism is a classic tautology, true by definition, but also amusingly absurd. The sentiment may be undeniable but it nevertheless seems profoundly pointless.

Sometimes the most obvious or seemingly banal statements are the ones that reveal the deepest truths. For instance, it is also true that a local congregation is a particular place, and its members live, work, shop, play, and otherwise exist in other, equally particular, places. But why would anyone make an observation as seemingly empty as that, much less base a book on it? Because, as we hope to show, place is an important dimension of the church's existence, one that has received little theological attention in spite—or because—of being so obvious.

Paradoxically, some of the most obvious place references in a congregation are to places distant in space and time: maps and relics of the Holy Land; church names from biblical places, such as Bethany, Bethel, Bethesda, Calvary, Elim, Gethsemane, Tabor, Zion; artifacts, traditions, and architectural motifs carried over from the congregation's ancestral homeland (for Lutherans, commonly Norway, Sweden, or Germany); support for missions, development, and relief activities in third-world countries; and connections to partner churches and synods in other countries.

At the other end of the spectrum, signals of place awareness are sharply focused on the church's property: construction or renovation of the church building; design and maintenance of the church grounds; greening the church to make its property, operations, and activities more environmentally aware and earth friendly—matters that often arouse strong feelings and political struggles within the congregation.

But churches must also attend to their relationship to the surrounding community: struggles of adjusting to changes in the age or ethnic demographics of the surrounding neighborhood or in the local economy; creating and/or supporting local outreach ministries such as food pantries or soup kitchens, free health clinics, homeless shelters and affordable housing initiatives, refugee resettlement programs, or tutoring and employment assistance. A congregation that has to consider closing its doors experiences deep grief at losing a familiar physical place saturated with communal history and personal memories. And special places other than the congregation play a role in the spiritual lives of at least some of the members, such as church camps, retreat centers, nursing homes, hospitals, cemeteries, or worship spaces other than the sanctuary—outside, on the church grounds or in a park.

Yet little attention has been paid to the dimension of place in thinking about the church's proclamation, ministry, and mission. Such attentiveness may seem irrelevant to or inessential for the church's real mission of proclaiming the gospel, or be dismissed as trivial and sentimental. The various outreach ministries by which a congregation connects itself to the life of its place may be disconnected from one another and categorized as "social" ministries in contrast to the "spiritual" ministries of worship, religious education, pastoral care, and so on. The ways in which a congregation connects to its location in social ministry or ecological stewardship are seldom subject to deep and sustained moral or theological reflection. To those involved, that these are simply good things to do is self-evident.

Embodied and Embedded

Nan listened attentively as her husband, Jeff, vented his growing frustrations as a parish pastor. Her response was simple, direct, and maddening: "You need a change." Jeff snapped back, "What difference

> will moving to another congregation make? The work and challenges of a parish pastor are the same wherever you go. The only thing that changes is the scenery!"

Many people try to minimize the implications that a change of scenery can have on their lives. Yet a change of scenery is more than window dressing we see only through our eyes; we experience it with our whole being. Most theological writing about the church has focused on its role in the individual's relationship to God and to other people. The physical location of the church has been regarded merely as a stage or backdrop, rather than having a unique character within God's redeemed creation and being a home place where God provides the resources for a congregation to fulfill its mission.

But if we take seriously the human condition to which the gospel is addressed, not to mention the doctrine of creation, we can hardly justify ignoring the fundamentally and inescapably "placed" character of the congregation as both proclaimer and hearer of the gospel. The church exists to communicate the gospel as the key to the ultimate meaning of human life. For Lutherans, the central meaning of faith is grace, the giftedness of creation and redemption. But as Lutherans, we often restrict grace to this latter dimension: we tend to center our faith on Christ's saving work, understood mainly as the grace of God that comes to each of us individually in the forgiveness of sins.

This is by no means wrong, but if that exhausts our understanding of God's grace and of what God is doing in our world, then we have lost the fullness of the biblical and Christian vision. The problem is not that we have misplaced the center of our faith, but that we have shrunk its circumference, impoverished its content, and dug a chasm between it and the world in which we live. That God is the Creator of the universe is not denied, but instead reduced to a footnote, an aside raised when environmental issues come up. Redemption is understood wholly in individual human terms as a subjective or post-mortem event—an antidote to guilt feelings, an analgesic to alleviate worldly suffering and anxiety, a ticket to a better place, or an escape from eternal punishment.

Insofar as it is *God's* grace, that meaning must be relevant to everything with which we have to do, for all things are related to God as the one "from whom are all things and for whom we exist" and to Christ as the one "through whom are all things and through whom we exist." (1 Cor. 8:6). To believe in God as Creator is not only to affirm God's role "in the beginning" of all things, but also to affirm God's continuing creative activity throughout the universe and in the innermost heart of every creature. God is therefore present and active—though hidden—in the whole context of our lives, wherever we find ourselves. As Paul proclaimed to the Athenians, "From one ancestor [God] made all nations to inhabit the whole earth, and he allotted the times of their existence and the boundaries of the places where they would live, that they would search for God and perhaps grope for him and find him—though indeed he is not far from each one of us. For, 'In him we live and move and have our being' . . ." (Acts 17:28). Or, in the psalmist's poignant cry, "Where can I go from your spirit? Or where can I flee from your presence? If I ascend to heaven, you are there; if I make my bed in Sheol, you are there. If I take the wings of the morning and settle at the farthest limits of the sea, even there your hand shall lead me, and your right hand shall hold me fast" (Ps. 139:7-10).

Insofar as it is God's grace *for us*, it must be related concretely to us as we are intimately bound up with our location in space and time, geography and history, ecology and society. We are not only embodied, we are embedded. We are not just persons, free-floating selves communing with other selves in some kind of void; we are persons-in-place. Our lives are not lived in isolation, or in a vacuum, or in a realm of interpersonal relationships and spiritual realities alone; our lives are lives-in-place. To live in a place is to live in relation to others who are also embodied and embedded—humans and nonhumans, animate or inanimate. These are our "neighbors" in the broadest possible sense of the term. Theologian H. Richard Niebuhr defined the neighbor whom we are to love as ourselves: "[The neighbor] is the near one and the far one; the one beside the road I travel here and now, the one removed from me by distances in time and space, in convictions and loyalties. . . . The neighbor is in past and present and future. . . . [The neighbor] is man and he is angel and he is animal and organic being, all that participates in being."[1] Thus, a place is defined not only by a boundary, but by a web of relationships between beings that share a common space. And it is also a nexus in a wider web of relationships that stretch around the globe and that connect us to past and future generations.

Space and Place

To understand how faith and place are related, we need to think more carefully about what *place* means. Places are spaces that have personal meaning for people, spaces that are charged with significance, good or bad. *Space* by itself is empty, abstract, general, and neutral—in contrast to the concrete, particular, filled, emotionally charged place. Space is usually something we try to get through as quickly as possible, a transition zone between places. Feeling under pressure to get more done in less time, with urban sprawl increasing the distances we go to work or shop, it seems that we experience our communities and landscapes more as spaces to traverse than places in which to dwell.

Taking time is essential for the perception of places, and for allowing our awareness of their layers of meaning to mature. The "slow food" movement, emerging in reaction to our eat-on-the-run culture of fast-food chain restaurants, encourages taking time to enjoy diverse, organically grown regional produce and traditional foods. Perhaps we need a "slow travel" movement that would promote getting around by walking, biking, or paddling in order to deepen a sense of place (and to reduce energy consumption and improve our health as well!). The slow travel movement would engage people with the question: "What difference will it make if you experience the area where you live at two to fifteen m.p.h. rather than fifty-five m.p.h.?" That faster pace gets us where we want to go more quickly, but slowness allows for deeper interaction with a place as well as between ourselves and God. Slow travel, or simply spending quiet, attentive time in a place, stimulates our senses, makes us mindful of its uniqueness, and moves us to praise the Creator.

A region of space becomes *place* when overlaid by particular values and meanings as a result of personal perceptions, feelings, and relationships that are connected with it. It is as if we placed a translucent overlay upon a map with varying colors, words, or symbols representing our knowledge, feelings, relationships, and associations concerning specific locations on that map. In terms of space, Yogi Berra was right: we are always somewhere, in terms of a spot you can find on a map or locate with a Global Positioning System. But that somewhere may not be a vital and meaningful place. There may be, as Gertrude Stein famously said of Oakland, "no *there* there."

A place can be any size, and can have many meanings, from the metaphorical to the literal, but we will be focusing—though not exclusively—on places as tangible, material, directly experienced geographical locations, with an emphasis on the local, on scales ranging roughly from a parcel of land (such as that occupied by a house and yard or church building and grounds) through a neighborhood to a community or metropolitan area. But at times we will refer to places on other scales as well, which we will specify or try to make clear from the context.

Place and Meaning

Places can have different sorts of meaning for people, in different ways.

Home. Places can be "home" on a vast range of scales, from the house or apartment where you live, to our city, state, or nation, or even the "home planet" Earth itself. What makes it a home? At a basic level, it is where we have ready and relatively unencumbered access to the necessities and comforts of life, and where we can retreat in privacy from exposure to the demands and scrutiny of the outside world. Association with a community or social network also plays a role: home is where we can connect with family, friends, and neighbors, balancing the need for privacy with the need for companionship. Feelings of at-homeness are also evoked by the stories and histories that are gathered around it: personal life stories, family histories, local community histories, or—on a planetary scale—the story of the emergence and development of life on earth.

The meaningfulness and necessity of having a home is set in sharp relief by the painful feelings associated with its absence: the vulnerability, discomfort, and loneliness that accompany being away from home and feeling out of place. Such feelings are even more intense and chronic for those who have no home at all to which they can return: the homeless, the refugee, the displaced person.

Identification. Closely related to a sense of a place as home are feelings of identification with, attachment to, or rootedness in that place. Without such feelings, even in those places where we live and that should feel like home, we may have the contrary experience of alienation and estrangement. But when we do have a sense of belonging to a place, we feel that we are part of its history, or that the character and history of that place is part of what makes us the persons we are. We may continue to identify with a place long after having left it—or even if we have never lived there at all—because it is part of our childhood or our family history, and we feel that we still carry a part of that place within us.

Use. But feelings of at-homeness or identification are not the only ways places can be meaningful for us. At a very pragmatic level, places may have significance for us because we are dependent upon them or find them useful for meeting our needs. The meaningfulness of some places for us consists in the presence of particular goods or benefits that bring us into contact with them: the workplace where we earn our income, the store or mall where we can get what we need, the clinic or service station, and so on. Conversely, we may relate to places as locations to avoid because of some threat or hazard to life and health we associate with it: the toxic waste site, the crime-infested neighborhood, the dangerous intersection.

Enjoyment. There are places that are meaningful or special to us because we enjoy them. We may value a certain place because we have an immediate emotional response to its beauty or majesty, or because we have an interest in and understanding of its unique natural or human past, the distinctive culture of its community, or the particular ecology of its landscape. Many different forms of knowledge—scientific, historical, sociological, and so on—can be brought to bear on a particular place, and each of them can enrich our appreciation and affection for it.

There are places that have negative significance for us as well, that repel rather than attract us because they are boring, tawdry, ugly, or unsettling. Although there are natural landscapes that have such effects on people, often such places are the result of human action, such as inappropriate "development" that mars the beauty of a natural landscape, or injustice and neglect that leads to urban blight. Their meaning may lie precisely in showing us what we do not want our places—and by extension our planet—to be or to become. Sometimes we have a clearer sense of what we *don't* want than what we *do* want, or we may better appreciate what we have when we have experienced what it would be like to lose it. And we may see in such disfigured landscapes a betrayal of their own best possibilities, lost opportunities for a more harmonious integration of humans and nature.

Responsibility. A place may be meaningful to us because we feel some responsibility for it. Because we enjoy it or depend on it, we may wish to preserve it for ourselves or others; we may feel that our ownership of it carries with it a custodial or stewardship responsibility to enhance, protect, or exercise care in our use of it. We may take a kind of proprietary interest in it because we have had some role in making or maintaining it.

On the other hand, we may not feel responsible for our place, especially places that lie outside our own household or workplace. It may be because of apathy or complacency, even selfishness, fed by a comfortable personal situation and an abundance of distractions and preoccupations: "Why rock the boat? Why get worked up? I'm doing all right." Or, any feelings of responsibility may be undercut by cynicism and despair because we feel we have no chance to make a difference. Our work and home responsibilities drain our time and energies. The community problems we hear about seem overwhelming and intractable. Without the opportunity and resources for effective participation, confronted by opposing forces simply too strong for us, we feel powerless, lacking the "ability" that is one prerequisite for responsibility (response-ability). And for many people, trapped by extreme poverty or social and political oppression or both, their power to affect their life-situation is severely limited, if not quite zero.

Spirituality. Finally, certain places can have particular spiritual meaning for us. There are some sites that are explicitly sacred, linked by communally shared symbols and stories to a larger religious context. Places hallowed by prayer, worship, and ritual: temples, mosques, cathedrals, synagogues, chapels, monasteries, sweat lodges. Sites of important events in the foundational narratives of a faith tradition: Sinai, Jerusalem, Bethlehem, Mecca, Uluru/Ayers Rock. Experiences of reverence, awe, peace, and inspiration give spiritual meaning to particular places and landscapes: an ocean shore, a forest path, a mountain, a churchyard. We often seek out such places, and bring others there, in quest of such experiences.

Spiritual meanings can be negative as well, threatening one's sense of harmony with the sacred. We may no longer believe the wilderness to be the chaotic, lawless abode of monsters and demons, as our medieval or Puritan forbears did. We may not regard big cities primarily as places where morality and piety are swallowed up by vice and iniquity, as past generations of rural and small-town folk did. Nonetheless, we may still find some wild or remote places strangely unsettling and "creepy," or feel a soul-numbing dread in a blighted urban area or industrial wasteland.

Grace and Place

The meaning of our lives can't be unrelated to the meaning of our places, and the meaning of all those with which we share that place. We are placed in grace, and graced in place. All places are therefore places in which we may encounter the grace of God—not only special holy places or sacred spaces, but ordinary, "secular" places as well. There is no sharp demarcation between "sacred" and "secular" or "not-sacred" places, as if a place either were spiritually meaningful or not. On the one hand, there are some particular places that evoke in us religious thoughts and feelings because of some association they may have with acts of worship or stories of faith. On the other hand, in faith we may know theoretically that God is present in and to all places in creation, but a more engaged experience of what that means *for us* in this or that particular place may be absent. We may not have an immediate sense of the holy in that place, but we can still respond to what we find there with appreciation, respect, care, and humility, knowing that we and they have a common grounding in the divine mystery. And, because all places are related to God, any place may become religiously meaningful *for us* when we recognize that relationship.

That recognition may come as the fruit of reflection and contemplation of a place that discloses the giftedness of what we encounter there; or it may be the result of an unlooked-for experience of the in-breaking of God's grace in an unlikely place. Nathaniel scoffed, "Can anything good come out of Nazareth?" (John 1:46). Matthew recalled the prophetic words: "And you, Bethlehem, in the land of Judah, are by no means the least among the rulers of Judah; for from you shall come a ruler who is to shepherd my people Israel" (Matt. 2:6). Or, as Jacob said upon waking from his dream at Bethel, "Surely the LORD is in this place—and I did not know it! . . . How awesome is this place! This is none other than the house of God, and this is the gate of heaven" (Gen. 28:16-17). Willie Nelson put it this way in his song "Yesterday's Wine": "Miracles appear in the strangest of places."

The meanings that a place can have for us gain a new dimension when considered as signs of God's grace in creation. To feel at home somewhere, to have roots in a place that nourish one's sense of selfhood; to be sustained by the beauty and fruitfulness of one's local landscape and the work and companionship of one's neighbors, can be experienced as holy gifts and occasions for gratitude and praise for God. In faith, we can see, in the chains of dependence and responsibility that link us to near and distant neighbors and to the whole earth community, our unique callings to serve Creator and creation in whatever places God has set us. To the eyes of faith, God not only reveals God's self to us in creation—through incarnation, word, sacrament—but God also reveals creation to us. We fully know creation's meaning and value when set in its relationship to God—namely, that it is a gift: gift of home or habitat, of wonder, of community.

All this talk about grace in creation does nothing to minimize the significance of the grace that came by Jesus Christ (John 1:17). Jesus is the revelation of God's graciousness, which grounds our faith that creation is in fact a place of grace, in spite of all experiences that seem to count against that belief. The assurance of God's grace in Jesus frees us from the anxiety that seeks security through exploiting and dominating our fellow creatures, human and nonhuman, who share our places. As the revelation of God, Christ stands in judgment over the idolatries to which our attachments to place may tempt us: parochialism, nationalism, ethnocentrism, isolationism, the elevation of "our way of life" to an absolute standard, and all the rest. Christ's resurrection means that the powers of death, destruction, and injustice do not have the last word, that we need not succumb to the temptations of inert despair or rash fanaticism, and that we can receive "faith to go forward with good courage, not knowing where we go, but only that [God's] hand is leading us and [God's] love supporting us . . ."[2]

Place as Vocation

Christian living is a matter of responding to all things in light of their relationship to God, responding to God's action on us through them, and serving God in all our interactions with them. To fail to relate God to some dimension of our life is to fail to acknowledge God as God. It is to divide our lives into compartments—some of them labeled "religious" or "spiritual" and some labeled "secular." But what that actually means is that those "secular" departments of our life will be handed over to some other source of value, some other "god"—one of the gods of pleasure or success, nation or tribe, image or ideology, culture or politics.

This is closely connected to the Lutheran idea of vocation. Vocation has traditionally meant that we serve God not only through special "religious" acts, such as prayer or Bible study or worship, but in our worldly callings in the family, civil government, or the economy. We serve God in our day-to-day activities as mothers and fathers, lawyers and launderers, doctors and drugstore clerks, teachers and technical support workers. What matters in Christian terms is not how "spiritual" an occupation is, or the status or salary it brings, but the opportunities it provides for serving the neighbor.

Similarly, because God encounters and acts on us not only in special "sacred" places but also in ordinary "secular" places, our interactions in and with any place are opportunities to respond to what God is doing there, and to what God intends for the people and things that are part of that place. Just as our occupational or family role is a "given" within which we are given certain definite possibilities for serving God and the neighbor by caring for this person—*our* child or *my* parent—or by carrying out this particular task or responsibility ("that's *my* job"), so our places represent particular given possibilities for serving God by communicating the grace of God, in word and deed, by caring for God's creation, human and nonhuman.

But it isn't just a matter of responsible action; our places are also opportunities for holy enjoyment of the mystery of the ordinary and profound appreciation for the wonder of the everyday, for encountering the multidimensional richness of the blessings that God has bestowed upon this earth. And they are places for grief and anger when we see relationships among inhabitants broken and distorted by injustice, or the betrayal of the promise of possibilities for a shared life on common ground. It is jarring, but not inconsistent, when Psalm 104, the great hymn to God as the Creator of habitat ("the earth is full of your creatures," v. 24b) ends: "I will sing to the Lord as long as I live. . . . Let sinners be consumed from the earth, and let the wicked be no more" (vv. 33a, 35a). There *should* be no place for sin and evil in the world—but alas, and in fact, there is.

Dis-graceful Places

As noted above, there are places that are *negatively* meaningful—that are alienating and suffocating, For too many of the world's people, the dominant reality may be that their places are materially, aesthetically, and spiritually impoverished and impoverishing, isolating, hazardous, and toxic. Places can be prisons, allowing little scope for fulfillment or for responsible action.

Often, the memories and stories that connect us to our places are those of moral failure. They may be personal memories of relationships that were broken or violated by ourselves or others; or collective sins of slavery, racism, displacement of native peoples, violence, or environmental degradation. They may be so deeply ingrained in these places that we cannot live there without being constantly reminded of those events, or without being enmeshed in their ongoing effects.

The forgiveness offered to us in Christ can free us to live with the awareness of past violations of the grace and goodness of creation, and to continue to serve God by caring for our places in full knowledge of their, and our, faults and failings. To say that creation is grounded in and suffused with God's grace is not to deny the reality of sin and evil. Grace may be refused or repudiated, its gifts rejected and misused. To see creation in the light of the grace we have encountered in Jesus Christ through Word and Sacrament is also to see creation under the sign of the cross. It is to recognize God's hiddenness in the world. It is to acknowledge our need for grace, our inability to live out of the resources—of ourselves or of the world—that we think we can claim and use as our own possessions. It is to lament as well as celebrate, and to recognize the limits as well as the moral necessity of human efforts.

Our ties to place themselves can be warped and twisted, made dysfunctional, destructive, and disgraceful. We can succumb to an idolatry of places, making them the source of grace rather than the field or medium within which grace is at work. We can become provincial or parochial, uninterested in and indifferent to what goes on in the "outside world"—at least, insofar as that is possible when even a small rural community is dependent on the vicissitudes of the global economy and vulnerable to distant polluters contaminating its air, water, food, or to toxic products from overseas factories. Nostalgia can divert us from attending to present-day problems, averting threats, adapting to inevitable changes, or adopting beneficial innovations. Pride can also lead us to overlook faults in ourselves and our places as well as the virtues of others. And, ugliest of all, a proper concern for the health and well-being of our places can become a virulent xenophobia—fear of the stranger—toward others whom we perceive as "undesirables" rather than as neighbors and fellow children of God: the poor, the homeless, the immigrant, those of different ethnic or cultural backgrounds, or anyone who is too different from our image of ourselves or our communities.

Each of these corruptions of a sense of place are idolatrous in that they tend to identify grace *only* with "our" place as it is known, familiar, or perceived by us, and fail to behold God's grace in the new and unfamiliar, or to exercise gracious hospitality toward the stranger. They are failures to recognize how the places in which the "common grace" of God in creation comes to us have the potential of becoming the means of that grace for "others" as well: "You shall not wrong or oppress a resident alien, for you were aliens in the land of Egypt" (Exod. 22:21); "When you reap the harvest of your land, you shall not reap to the very edges of your field, or gather the gleanings of your harvest. You shall not strip your vineyard bare, or gather the fallen grapes of your vineyard; you shall leave them for the poor and the alien: I am the LORD your God" (Lev. 19:9-10). And they are failures to realize how the "other" as neighbor, as a part and participant in our place, can become a conduit of grace *for us:* "Do not neglect to show hospitality to strangers, for by doing that some have entertained angels without knowing it" (Heb. 13:2).

But faith in God as Creator is faith that grace is the fundamental reality, that evil is nothing more than the corruption of something that is originally and essentially good; to believe in God as Redeemer is to believe that healing and restoration, however incomplete, can happen anywhere—and is needed everywhere.

Cultivating Grace

These meanings become realized in individual and congregational practices that can be described, metaphorically and literally, as cultivation. Cultivation—the transformation of nature in accordance with purposes and values—is part of the human vocation. Human presence and activity, as described in Genesis, adds something to the given creation.

Adam is placed in the garden to "till" it (Gen. 2:15). But consider the back-story of God's creation of humanity:

> In the day that the LORD made the earth and the heavens, when no plant of the field was yet in the earth and no herb of the field had yet sprung up—for the LORD God had not caused it to rain upon the earth, and there was no one to till the ground; but a stream would rise from the earth, and water the whole face of the ground—then the

> Lord God formed man from the dust of the ground, and breathed into his nostrils the breath of life and the man became a living being. (Gen. 2:4b-7)

The land needs someone to cultivate it, and evidently Adam is formed from the earth to meet that need, just as the stream rises up to water it. The word normally translated "till" or "cultivate" literally means "serve." The garden thus served by both the water and the human is both beautiful and fruitful: "And the Lord God planted a garden in Eden, in the east; and there he put the man whom he had formed. Out of the ground the Lord God made to grow every tree that is pleasant to the sight and good for food . . ." (Gen. 2:8-9).

Human cultivation brings out the earth's latent potentialities for life and beauty. We can understand "cultivation" in a broad sense, as including not only farming and gardening but also all human transformations of nature—construction, crafts and technology, art and architecture, music, manufacturing, and so on. It is not that the earth entirely lacks beauty or fruitfulness without us. And it is not that we somehow "improve on" nature, as if it were defective and needed our correction. Rather, human activity completes creation, or perhaps it would be better to say culture complements nature.

But Adam is also given the task of "keeping" the garden. We complement or add to the garden of nature even as we protect and preserve it. The values we create supplement, but do not abolish or override, the goodness that, as we know from Genesis 1, is already there. The fulfillment of our vocation to cultivate is not the transformation of the whole of nature, or the production of a wholly domesticated world. The result of cultivation that respects nature would be a relationship that enhances both nature and cultivator, and that yields a good that is more than the sum of the separate goods of its parts.

But our cultural products add to nature in yet another way: through images and ideas that are not embodied in our material artifacts and physical creations. The third task given to Adam is that of naming the animals (Gen. 2:19). This introduces into humans' relationship to nature the element of language—and, by extension, all the things we do with language: poetry and song, myth making and storytelling, prayer and theology, philosophy and science, politics and dialogue, and so on. Through language and thought we relate ourselves to the world around us by labeling, classifying, organizing, describing, praising, complaining, asking questions, imagining possibilities, making plans, and many other activities that may take place in conversation with others or inside our own heads.

For human beings, language is the medium of meaning. Thus, language—especially telling stories and relating history—is a crucial element in the transformation of space into place. Recollecting the congregation's story provides a helpful foundation and place to begin this transformation. A congregation's sense of place deepens by remembering its history. The stories about moving from a former site to a new site, or from homelessness to home are as important to the identity of a congregation as they were to the Israelites who journeyed from slavery in Egypt and wandered through the wilderness before venturing into a land promised by God. What do these stories tell us about the determination and convictions of a congregation? The Israelites' move into the promised land was met with resistance. What were the congregation's challenges in securing a place to call home: red tape, financial struggles, differences of opinion, resistance of neighbors? These stories have the potential to inspire future generations in the challenges they face and kindle gratitude for both the place to call home and the people who led them there.

A Story of Place

Madison Christian Community was founded on a vision for an ecumenical partnership and the generosity of a farm family named Dauk. Two brothers, Herman and Gilman, with their wives and children, were the second generation on the family farm. When they decided to sell the land to a housing developer they wanted to ensure that the people who would move to the area would have a place of worship. They went to their pastor, Jim Ohlrogge, at St. Luke's Lutheran Church in Middleton, Wisconsin, and shared their hope of giving a parcel of land for the purpose of establishing a new congregation. Pastor Ohlrogge facilitated the process that led to the Dauks's gifting seven acres of land to MCC. The church building that was constructed included a cylindrical tower resembling a silo, in remembrance of the farm that had once been there. The Dauks's generous gift of land is a story that evokes gratitude among MCC members and inspires them to respond to God's abundance by generously sharing their gifts within the congregation and beyond, in the community.

Every congregation has a story about its place, and every place has a prehistory that comes before the wave of European immigrants settled in North America with their religious traditions. A study of a congregation's prehistory considers the native people, plants and animals, terrain and geology of the place and makes connections with the present life of a congregation. When MCC added a second sanctuary to its original building, the topsoil was mounded in the shape of a bird, and prairie grass seeds were sown on it, as a symbolic recognition of the congregation's prehistory and to honor both the land and the people who relied upon that land for their life and well-being.

Every summer for the past thirty-five years MCC high school youth travel to northern Minnesota to canoe in the Boundary Waters. Once a park warden visited the group at its campsite and, learning they were from southern Wisconsin, asked, "Do you realize that thousands of years ago glaciers picked up the topsoil from this area and carried it hundreds of miles south, to places like southern Wisconsin?" We often recall this story when on our hands and knees planting seed, pulling weeds, or picking produce in MCC's garden. It is marvelous to think that the Boundary Waters is not only a scenic place four hundred miles to the north, but is also as close as the soil in a garden providing nutrients for a seed to root, grow, and produce vegetables. Given this, how can we not give thanks to God who unites heaven and earth, north and south, seed and soil? Learning the history and prehistory of a place deepens a congregation's appreciation and connection to people of past generations, creation, and God.

* * *

Humans' culture-creating activities are part of God's intention for creation. Clearly we haven't done so well in cultivating good lives in good places. Many of the places we have made, and the way we have made them, are dehumanizing and environmentally destructive. Contemporary American society is characterized by lifestyles, values, and beliefs that alienate us from nature, weaken the bonds of community, and diminish our ties to place. Still, cultural creativity is part of our calling as humans. We do have the potential for dwelling more gracefully and graciously on earth.

And we'd better—for it is a matter of survival:

> I [the LORD God] call heaven and earth to witness against you today that I have set before you life and death, blessings and curses. Choose life so that you and your descendants may live, loving the LORD you God, obeying him, and holding fast to him; for that means life to you and length of days, so that you may live in the land that the LORD swore to give to your ancestors, to Abraham, to Isaac, and to Jacob. (Deut. 30:19-20)

Questions for Reflection and Discussion

1. Think of a place that has been particularly important in your own life. How would you describe it in physical terms—how it registers on your five senses? What feelings do you associate with being there? What do you know about its history, ecology, or culture? How has the place changed in the time you've known it? Is it currently threatened with degradation or destruction in any way? How would your own life have been different without that place?

2. As you think about the place where you live now, what do you especially value about it?

3. What factors in your life—particularly your faith—help or hinder your having a strong sense of place?

4. What are the "disgraceful places" in your community that need an infusion of grace?

2

Earth to Earth: The Material Culture of the Congregation

> Ashes to ashes, dust to dust. . . . Remember that you are dust, and to dust you shall return.
>
> —*Evangelical Lutheran Worship*[1]

These are the words we say over the deceased at funerals and to congregants as the ashes are placed on their foreheads at Ash Wednesday services. Yet "earth to earth" might be as appropriate a formula to remind us of our individual trajectories from soil to "living soul" (Gen. 2:7, KJV) and back to soil. It is a trajectory we share with other living things, as Psalm 104 declares: "When you [God] open your hand, they are filled with good things . . . when you take away their breath, they die and return to their dust" (vv. 28b, 29b). The same is true of our buildings and other products, though the formula may never have been spoken at a church's demolition. But "earth to earth" applies to the church's daily operations as well, for it involves a flow of materials and energy—water, electricity, food, paper—from the environment and back into it again.

The church's building, grounds, and use of material resources are the most visible, direct, and concrete ways that a congregation relates itself to its place and to the rest of creation. They are a good place for beginning to think through how a congregation embodies and embeds itself in its place.

In present-day America, a church building is usually a construction of wood, brick, stone, concrete, steel, and glass, perhaps set on a landscaped suburban plot of land with grass, trees, flowers, shrubbery, and a parking lot, or embedded in a downtown city block surrounded by cement, asphalt, and other buildings. An anthropologist or archaeologist would classify it as an artifact or a piece of *material culture.* That is, it is a physical object intentionally shaped by human beings out of raw materials taken from the earth for purposes that might be utilitarian, aesthetic, or religious or some combination thereof.

Theologically speaking, the church's physical form is an expression of the gift of human creativity, a product of architectural artistry and engineering skill. It is an example of the first two forms of culture described in chapter 1—the creation of distinctively human-made objects that stand out from the natural world, and the transformation of the landscape by changing its contours and the assortment of species that live on it.

If the design and operation of the congregation's physical plant is really to be in keeping with our human vocation as culture-producing creatures, we need to understand how human creations mesh or fail to mesh with God's creation. In biblical terms, this means living by God's wisdom in our dealings with our human neighbors and with the natural world. One of the antiphons appointed for use during Advent addresses Christ as Wisdom: "O Wisdom, proceeding from the mouth of the Most High, pervading and permeating all creation, mightily ordering all things: Come and teach us the way of prudence."[2]

Prudence and wisdom mean, in part, paying attention to the given structure of creation. Here, Scripture can give us important insights: not as a substitute for scientific investigation and careful reflection on our experience of successful and unsuccessful ways of living on earth, but as pointing to aspects of our world to which we must attend, honor, and safeguard. Within this general orientation of respect for the values that are inherent in creation as God's handiwork, secular knowledge and practical experience can be valuable sources of more detailed guidance and insight.

Creation as a Home for Life

As we build and manage our houses of worship, we need to bear in mind that creation is God's gift of a life-sustaining home for all creatures. This theme is especially clear in Genesis 1 and Psalm 104.

The opening verses of the Bible tell how God has created space for life, a habitat within which a variety of forms of life can flourish. If we look at the Genesis creation story, we can notice an important pattern to the sequence of six days. On the first day, light is created and separated from the darkness to create day and night. On the second day, God makes the dome of the sky (the "firmament") to separate the waters above the dome from the waters below the dome, so that beneath the sky is the open space of the air, and below that the vast expanse of water. On the third day, the land emerges as God gathers the waters under the sky into one place as the seas, and vegetation appears on the land. Thus, on the first three days, creation is separated into distinct zones or spaces.

Over the next three days, God populates each space with its appropriate inhabitants. The sun, moon, and stars are created on the fourth day to rule over the day and the night. On the fifth day, the birds of the air and the fish and other creatures of the sea are created to fill their respective spaces. And on the sixth day, the animals—including wild animals, domestic animals ("cattle"), "creeping things," and human beings—are created to dwell on the land. A place for everything, and everything in its place.

At a smaller scale, we find a similar attention to the relationship of creatures and habitats in Psalm 104. "By the streams the birds of the air have their habitation. . . . the stork has its home in the fir trees, the high mountains are for the wild goats; the rocks are a refuge for the coneys" (vv. 12a, 17b-18). Creatures, both earthbound and celestial, have their places in time as well: "You [God] have made the moon to mark the seasons; the sun knows its time for setting. You make darkness, and it is night, when all the animals of the forest come creeping out. The young lions roar for their prey, seeking their food from God. When the sun rises, they withdraw and lie down in their dens. People go out to their work and to their labor until the evening" (vv. 19-23).

Elsewhere in the Bible, human communities, too, are seen as having been given their living spaces by God. Not only Israel and the "promised land," but as Paul tells the Athenians, "From one ancestor [God] made all nations to inhabit the whole earth, and he allotted the times of their existence and the boundaries of the places where they would live . . ." (Acts 17:26).

Although we may not operate with the same picture of the cosmos as did the biblical writers, we can still appreciate the earth as the gift of a zone in which conditions are right for life to flourish, as well as the gifts of our particular places and habitats. Through our construction of homes and other buildings to house our activities, our reshaping of the face of the earth through landscaping, agriculture and forestry, urbanization, and road building, we humans create homes for ourselves within the larger household of creation. Human cultivation of creation must be ordered by wisdom that respects the limits and integrity of creation—the order and laws that govern the home for life that God has created.

A congregation must therefore recognize its embeddedness in the interdependent fabric of its social and natural environment, and ensure that what it does with building, grounds, and operations help to maintain the local and global environment as a fit home for human and other forms of life. The congregation's attention to its impact on the social and economic environment can be a model for its members in their own homes, workplaces, and communities.

The Church as an Organism and Environment

The connection between a congregation's building and creation leads us to compare the building to an organism. Granted, human and non-human organisms are more intricate and wondrous. But a building, like an organism, is dependent upon creation for water, fuel, light, and air. A building has the equivalent of a nervous (electrical) and digestive (plumbing) system. Furthermore, the building releases by-products into the environment, such as wastewater into the sewage system and carbon dioxide and other pollutants into the atmosphere. Human engineering and creation's cycles intersect as natural resources are converted for human usage. This is true not only for electrical and plumbing systems, but also for the church's physical setting and the materials used to construct and furnish it. Unfortunately, our buildings and the human-made systems that support them seldom participate in natural cycles in ways that will sustain creation over the long term.

Just as we easily take water for granted, it is easier yet for a congregation to take its building and grounds for granted. Buildings and grounds do not suffer from neglect as much as from disconnection from creation. Not only do we overlook their dependence on inputs from the environment, but we also forget that they—like all organisms—are also part of the environment for other creatures.

Assessing the impact of a congregation's building upon the environment requires a deliberate act of consciousness raising and commitment, similar to the confession of faith in the order of baptism. The baptismal confession includes a threefold renunciation: "Do you renounce the devil and all their forces that defy God . . . the powers of this world that rebel against God. . . . the ways of sin that draw you from God?" And it includes, conversely, a threefold affirmation: "Do you believe in God the Father . . . Do you believe in Jesus Christ, the Son of God . . . Do you believe in God the Holy Spirit?"[3]

Let us begin with the renunciations: Do you renounce the unnecessary use of nonrenewable sources of energy? Do you renounce the use of nonrecyclable materials that are disposed of in landfills and take thousands of years to decompose? Do you renounce the use of toxic cleaning chemicals and lawn fertilizers that are detrimental to human and nonhuman life?

Many congregations have taken significant steps in this process of renunciation by making their buildings more energy efficient; making greater use of renewable energy; recycling and purchasing supplies made from recycled materials; using nontoxic, biodegradable cleaners; and by more environmentally friendly lawn care or replacing lawns with natural landscaping that requires less water and chemicals. We can see the theological significance of these activities by connecting them to the congregation's sacramental life and evangelical witness. Water use and energy conservation provide two concrete, practical examples.

Water and Baptism

The integral relationship between a congregation and the environment is oftentimes diminished or neglected because of the tendency to focus upon the congregation as a group of people in relationship to God and one another. For example, theorists provide insightful connections between family systems and the healthy or unhealthy ways congregations function. But all systems—economic, political, and social—exist within the context of creation. They contribute either to creation's enhancement or to its degradation. Creation flourishes or withers; and the condition of creation, in turn, has an impact on those same systems. Congregations that tend to their relationship with creation, as well as to their relationship with God and one another, embrace a more robust trinitarian theology—one that affirms "God the Father Almighty, maker of heaven and earth;" Jesus Christ, "through [whom] all things were made," and "the Holy Spirit, the Lord, the giver of life" (Nicene Creed).

The baptismal liturgy expresses just such a trinitarian theology, articulating how the sacrament places the baptized in a web of spiritual, social, and ecological connections. In the sacrament of baptism, "we are reborn children of God."[4] A biblical understanding of baptism teaches that we are united to Christ in a death like his, and in a resurrection like his (Rom. 6:5). We are connected with one another and made members of the body of Christ through baptism. The flood prayer in the order of baptism connects the baptized community to creation, beginning with these words: "We give you thanks, O God, for in the beginning your Spirit moved over the waters and by your Word you created the world, calling forth life in which you took delight."[5]

But we easily overlook the real significance of water in connecting us to creation, both in baptism and in our daily lives. As Mark Hanson, Presiding Bishop of the ELCA, writes, "I take water for granted and assume there will be clean water for drinking and cooking, warm water for cleansing and fresh water for our garden. My travels have shaken me out of complacency, however. When I witness women walking for hours and then standing in line to fill a bucket with water, I realize both the precious gift and human necessity of water."[6]

The tap water that fills a pitcher and is carried into the sanctuary and poured into the baptismal font is also water that is taken for granted. To take something "for granted" is the opposite of regarding something as a gift. A gift is received with gratitude and humility; that which is taken for granted is taken thoughtlessly, as no more than one's due. The psalmist celebrates water as God's gift to the living creation: "You make springs gush forth in the valleys; they flow between the hills, giving drink to every wild animal. . . . From your lofty abode you water the mountains; the earth is satisfied with the fruit of your work" (Ps. 104:10-11a, 13).

Perhaps a flow chart of the water system should be placed near every baptismal font. The water is pumped from a sandstone aquifer several hundred feet below the surface into a water tower. Chlorine and fluoride are added to the water. The water in the tower is carried by the flow of gravity to a water main. A building's plumbing system connects with a water main and water flows into a building to be controlled by kitchen faucets, showerheads, and toilet handles. The water that fills the baptismal font travels some distance, but it still participates in the water cycles of creation. And if warm water is used, there should also be a flow chart of the energy system, tracing the electricity or natural gas that warms the water back through the church building to the power plant or distribution and processing systems and the renewable or nonrenewable resources used to generate the electricity, or the well from which the gas came.

Why pay so much attention to the water used in baptism? Because matter matters. In baptism, God uses a common, ordinary part of our environment to convey to us the life-giving power of Christ's life, death, and resurrection. In the sacrament of baptism, the spiritual and the material are united in the means of grace. Luther notes how God's Word and water are connected in the sacrament: "Baptism is not simply plain water. Instead it is water used according to God's command and connected with God's Word."[7] At the same time, baptism is not by words alone, but by Word with the same water that circulates through the biosphere sustaining humans, plants, and animals.

Energy and Evangelism

In 2005 Madison Christian Community became one of four congregations to receive the Congregation Energy Star Award from the U.S. Department of Energy.[8] This award was in recognition of MCC's efforts to reduce its energy consumption over a period of four years, wherein they reduced emissions into the atmosphere by 40 percent, or 22,400 pounds of carbon dioxide per year.

This effort began when MCC organized a "Windmill Task Force" to explore the feasibility of placing a small wind generator on the church's site. The task force quickly learned of two issues that need to be taken into account before beginning a serious discussion about using a renewable energy source such as wind power.

First, the building needs to undergo a top-to-bottom energy assessment, including an energy audit to determine how much energy is being used by everything that requires electricity. This information is useful in determining whether energy-efficient replacements and modifications in usage are feasible and cost effective. Oftentimes, energy-saving materials cost more up front, but also tend to save money over a payback period of months or years because they allow the church to use less energy and save on heat and electricity bills. However, a congregation's commitment to care for creation by reducing its energy consumption should be as highly valued as saving money. If a thorough assessment is done before a crisis occurs, then a congregation is more likely to take energy conservation into account and less likely to choose the least expensive way to address the matter at hand.

Second, the monthly billing statement from the power and light company provides important historical data on energy use, including monthly and yearly utility charges for peak demand usage. From this one can see a strong correlation between church activities—meetings, Bible and book studies, prayer and quilting groups, worship and fellowship—and energy consumption.

Imagine a potluck dinner immediately following Sunday morning worship. The lights in the sanctuary are left on because people are milling around and visiting, and nobody has remembered to turn off the sound system. All the fluorescent lights are on in fellowship hall and slow cookers, roasters, and coffeepots are plugged into every outlet. Buns are warming in the oven and someone is going to start the dishwasher so the booster heater is ready for a speedy clean-up. Hopefully, everyone has a very good time, because the congregation will likely be paying a surcharge in next month's energy bill, and if this is the highest usage in the past twelve months they may also be paying a peak demand charge until the next potluck dinner rolls around.

Useful information from the energy assessment and the review of past energy bills will lead a congregation to examine its energy consumption habits and modify behaviors to reduce its overall use of energy. Such actions not only reduce the monthly costs but also reduce the peak demand, resulting in further energy savings. A sign is posted on the kitchen wall right above the industrial dishwasher at MCC asking, "Is this a good time to run the dishwasher? Yes, if the lights and sound systems are turned off in the Blessing Room and Covenant Room. No, if the room is occupied with people." And how about those huge coffeepots that are filled with water and plugged in first thing on Sunday morning? If coffee is prepared an hour before congregants arrive and most lights are turned off, the coffee can be poured into insulated containers, which will keep it warm for hours. And if the coffee is "fair trade," justice will never have tasted better!

Now, the congregation can finally research the use of alternative, renewable sources of energy. Many rural churches are located on a hilltop where the wind is steady and strong. A church roof is a potential site for a hot water or photovoltaic solar unit. Geothermal systems use the earth's natural ability to store heat to provide warmth in the winter and cooling in the summer. A feasibility study will help to determine whether such an alternative energy source is realistic. Fiscally responsible members of a congregation will raise the question of how many years of energy savings will make it worth spending the extra money up front, so a cost analysis is in order. It is important to inquire about rebates and grants from the power company or state agencies for using renewable energy. Even if a cost analysis shows that the congregation may not recover its investment, the cost to the environment of *not* using renewable energy must be taken into account. When a congregation chooses to use renewable sources of energy it is making a public witness to the community.

The wind analysis done for MCC showed that, even though its site is open and elevated above the surrounding neighborhood, it is a marginal location for a wind generator. But a surprising revelation was that the building is perfectly situated for a photovoltaic unit. The windmill task force learned of an organization that awarded grants up to $15,000 to install renewable energy technology. One question on the grant application asked about the potential for replicating the project. The answer: thousands of church roofs are ready and waiting for a photovoltaic unit in every city across the land! Another question inquired about the visibility of the project in the community. The city transportation department reported that more than eleven thousand cars drive past this site on an average day. The church was awarded a demonstration grant, and the unit was installed. A special outdoor service was held to dedicate the solar panels.

The most frequently asked question is, "How much of the building's energy usage is provided by the photovoltaic unit?" The bottom line is a meager 5 percent, but the better answer is, "It depends." It depends upon the activity in the building, the length of the day, and the season of the year. The photovoltaic unit provides up to 80 percent of the energy from Monday through Saturday during the summer months when building usage is less than the other seasons. And conversely, the photovoltaic unit produces much less energy during the winter months when the days are shorter and the snow piles up on the roof.

But more important is the fact that the photovoltaic unit on the roof of the building is a visible witness to every person who passes by that the congregation is committed to reducing its use of nonrenewable sources of energy. Many people who become members cite the congregation's care for the environment as a primary reason for joining. The addition of the photovoltaic unit has been a major reason the congregation is identified as one that cares for creation.

Affirmations for the Church on Earth

By seeking to conserve energy, use it more efficiently, and adopt renewable sources of energy, a congregation renounces the idea that we are entitled to consume natural resources without limit even if it means spoiling the earth as God's gift of an abode for life. Such renunciation is a way of living into our baptisms, but is possible only on the basis of fundamental, positive affirmations by the congregation about the Creator and the creation.

The first affirmation for a congregation is: "Do you affirm the relationship between God and nonhuman life that exists independently of human life?" Christians have often claimed that only human beings matter to God, and that God created everything else only for the sake of human beings. The Bible, however, indicates otherwise. God asks Job from the whirlwind, "Who has cut a channel for the torrents of rain . . . to bring rain on a land where no one lives, on the desert, which is empty of human life, to satisfy the waste and desolate land, and to make the ground put forth grass?" (Job 38:25-27). Recall that, in Genesis 1, God sees that creation is good, and blesses the birds and fishes, even before humans appear on the scene.

The second affirmation is, "Do you affirm the mutual support of human and nonhuman life in praising God?" In worship, we are called to "sing with all the people of God, and join in the hymn of all creation."[9] Psalm 148 comprises perhaps the widest range of God-praising voices in all of Scripture: "Praise him, all his angels . . . sun and moon . . . shining stars . . . sea monsters and all deeps, fire and hail, snow and frost, stormy wind . . . Mountains and all hills, fruit trees and all cedars! Wild animals and all cattle, creeping things and flying birds! Kings of the earth and all peoples . . . Young men and women alike, old and young together!" (vv. 2, 3, 7-12). In Psalm 104, it is the human psalmist who praises God on behalf of the rest of creation. Biblical scholar Terence Fretheim writes, "In George Herbert's language, human beings have been made the secretaries of the praise of nature. Without the praise of the nonhuman, the witness of the human would not be what it has the potential of becoming. . . . We live in a world highly charged with wonder and praise; it is up to human beings to give it clearer voice."[10]

And third, "Do you affirm the human's role to bring earthly orders to their fullest potential?" In chapter 1, we noted that humans, creatively cooperating with nature, can realize creation's latent possibilities for beauty and goodness. Among these are new possibilities for creation's praise of God. To quote Fretheim again: "Positively, the human being is needed to bring at least the earthly orders to their fullest possible potential, and that would entail their fullest possible potential for praise. There remains work to be done in the natural world by human beings in order for this potential to be more fully realized (see Genesis 2:5)."[11]

A Place for Nature's Praise of God

These three affirmations can prompt a congregation to enhance its immediate environment for the sake of nature's praise of God. Acting on the basis of positive affirmation is an alternative to fear-driven motives to "save the world." Fear-driven motives—though justifiable given the grave condition of creation—are difficult to sustain, for avoiding disaster is the best we can hope for. On the other hand, working directly with the earth sensitizes us to the fact that, though marred by humans,

> . . . nature is never spent;
> There lives the dearest freshness deep down things; . . .
> Because the Holy Ghost over the bent
> world broods with warm breast and with ah! bright wings.[12]

We catch the persistent, if faint, strains of creation's praise of God and experience our own ability to release and amplify it. With such positive reinforcement, our resolve to care for creation is strengthened.

Church-growth proponents recognize the importance of a congregation's "curb appeal." The congregation's property needs to be inviting and welcoming: visible signage listing the congregation's name and time of worship; adequate outdoor lighting that says "We're home and waiting up for you" to the public; adequate parking located near the building's handicap accessible entrance; and so on. These are important considerations, but how the landscape surrounding the building enhances creation to the praise of God is equally important.

Perhaps the old saying, "Beauty is in the eye of the beholder," holds true for the way we view landscape. But we will do well to pause and consider how our perceptions of beauty are shaped and influenced. Sometime between the garden of Eden and *Better Homes and Gardens* we've bought into the notion that a lawn is not beautiful unless it is weed free, perpetually green, and well trimmed and manicured. "Thou shalt have a green lawn" may be the American way, or the message from fertilizer and lawn-care companies, but Scripture witnesses to the beauty of creation's diversity: "The pastures of the wilderness overflow, the hills gird themselves with joy, the meadows clothe themselves with flocks, the valleys deck themselves with grain, they shout and sing together for joy" (Ps. 65:12-13).

"The Church with the Prairie"

Madison Christian Community is known in the surrounding neighborhoods as "the church with the prairie out front." Part of the property has been filled with prairie plantings that include, in addition to varieties of grasses, prairie smoke, baptisia, bush clover, lespedezia, yellow and purple coneflower, bergamot, goldenrod, and asters. A brochure about "The Prairie of the Madison Christian Community" expresses a sense of responsibility—and hospitality—informed by a historical and ecological perspective on the church's land:

> Native Wisconsin prairie plants again grow on a small restored prairie at the Madison Christian Community. As part of our mission to care for our world, this prairie preserves a part of the natural diversity that thrived before white settlers came to this part of southern Wisconsin. It provides cover for small mammals and birds that are losing their habitat as the west side of Madison develops. Walking in this small prairie, we can experience the land as our ancestors did when they first saw this "sea of grass." . . . We are committed to providing a space for plants that have been in our land for thousands of years . . .

> Maintaining the prairie since 1983 has been a cooperative effort by members of the Madison Christian Community. Some helped to hand-gather the seeds from remnant prairies along railroad track and from "goat prairies", hillsides too steep to cultivate. In the spring the members burn the prairie to stimulate native plants and control non-native species.[13]

Without suggesting that every congregation can or should do exactly as MCC has done, we recommend that congregations think about their property and the programs therein as a place where members can grow into a deeper sense of understanding for, appreciation of, and wonder at creation. Flowers, shrubs, and leaves of trees bloom into a marvelous array of colors and their beauty both praises God and moves those who notice to praise God. In the same way, the colors of a pastor's stole, liturgical banners, and altar cloths change with the seasons of the church year and each color holds symbolic meaning. Noting that the liturgical colors are rooted in the colors of creation can lead us to make the same symbolic connections in places outside the building as we do in the building.

Habitat and Hospitality

Cultivating a God-praising diversity of native plants on the church grounds expresses another aspect of an appreciation for creation as the gift of a home for all creatures—that of hospitality. Congregations exercise the virtue of hospitality in the many ways they open their place to "others": warmly welcoming visitors and new members; making its facilities accessible to persons with disabilities; providing space for a homeless shelter or food pantry; assisting with refugee resettlement; reaching out to persons of a different race, economic class, ethnicity, or sexual orientation. The exercise of hospitality is an essential practice for counteracting the xenophobia and fortress mentality that can infect a congregation's strong identification with and attachment to its property.

Hospitality, for a congregation, is not only about welcoming people; it's also about welcoming a diversity of plants and animals by providing habitat. As is usually the case with the practice of hospitality, there are tensions and ambivalence. Rabbits and gophers nibble away at MCC's gardens, but occasionally they attract the attention of a hawk, whose graceful flight is a rare pleasure in an urban environment.

Diverse, beautiful, and natural landscaping extends the congregation's ministry of place in other ways, by providing the neighborhood with opportunities for refreshment, reflection, and enjoyment of nature; natural cleansing of the water and air; reduced air pollution from lawn mowing; and less water pollution from lawn fertilizer and pesticides. Even congregations with little or no land can find space for potted plants or container gardens, bat houses or bird feeders, vermiculture bins where worms turn kitchen scraps into compost, or artwork and photographs that reflect and celebrate whatever makes their part of creation special.

The building and grounds of every church is both an organism—exchanging energy and materials with its surroundings—and an environment—contributing living space of good or poor quality to human beings, plants, and animals. When we recognize that fact, we can shape or reshape them to the glory and service of the Creator who has fashioned this marvelous planet as a home for myriad forms of life—and in so doing, live out our human vocation as cultivators and keepers of the earth.

Questions for Reflection and Discussion

1. How does your church relate to the environment and creation?

2. Are there any renunciations and affirmations that you would add or remove from the list above?

3. How does the landscape around your church lead to or detract from deeper appreciation and reflection on the wonder of creation?

4. How does the understanding of hospitality presented above expand or challenge your own understanding?

3

Cultivating Christians: Worship and Education

> [The righteous] are like trees planted by streams of water,
> Which yield their fruit in due season and their leaves do not wither.
> —Ps. 1:3

> I [Paul] planted, Apollos watered, but God gave the growth.
> —1 Cor. 3:6

The reason the congregation needs a physical structure is to house the activities that define it: the gathering of Christians to hear the Word, receive the sacraments, and to grow and mature in the ability to understand and live their faith. So we must also rethink the activities of worship and education in relation to the congregation's particular place within creation.

Christians are not members of a religious club. They are disciples in the making, growing as embodied and embedded members of Christ's body in the world (Eph. 4:15-16), as those who are becoming "new creatures" in Christ (2 Cor. 5:17). This, too, is a matter of cultivation, of the formation and nurture of persons' inner lives in and by the congregation. How might the congregation's place play a role in Christian formation, and how could being formed in Christian faith transform Christians' relationships to their places?

The Congregation in Three Dimensions

As the concrete, material setting of worship and education, the congregation stands at the intersection of the dimensions of personal identity, space, and time. It is at this intersection that it can cultivate in its members awareness, appreciation, and responsibility for their place in creation, and consciousness of how that place enters into their relationships to God and neighbor.

Gathering Place

The Greek New Testament word for church is *ekklesia*, meaning "called out." While this is usually thought of religiously, as denoting a people set apart by a particular faith identity, it can also be interpreted geographically. When the congregation gathers for worship, its members are called out from their varied and scattered places into a particular place. The gathering of the congregation establishes a physical space or a frame into which the meanings and symbols of Christian faith are introduced in visual or verbal form. Here a cross or crucifix is displayed, an altar or communion table is set up, the Word is preached, hymns are sung, candles are lit, the baptismal font is filled, banners and paraments are hung. While almost any suitable meeting place—indoors or out—can house the assembly, what we usually think of as "worship space" is a church building.

The distinctive symbols involved in worship, whether part of a permanent structure or temporarily set up in a borrowed space, and the rituals performed there, serve to distinguish the sacred space of worship from ordinary space.[1] But the distinction cannot be absolute, for the ordinary world itself, as God's creation, also has a sacred dimension. How a church expresses a living and religiously significant connection to its geographical context is a more subtle matter. Older churches may stand at the current or former literal or symbolic center of the town. The presence of a cemetery links the adjacent church to the community's history and the residents' life-cycles. The building's design and materials may deliberately reflect the local landscape and culture.

The spatial character of the typical congregation as both different from and related to its surrounding environment reflects parallel dialectics in the other two dimensions, those of personal identity and time.

Gathered People

Those who are gathered—the literal meaning of *congregation*—as the church are given a sacred identity: they are disciples called to follow Christ in the particular places of their lives. As those who are being redeemed, they are not saved *out* of or *apart* from the world. Rather, their redemption is a matter of being freed *from* the world *for* the world. The gathering or assembly in a particular place is a physical and spatial symbol of the "freedom *from*" the world that is part of the double liberation required for Christian discipleship.

We are freed *from* the world in the sense of being liberated from bondage to cultural values and social practices that run contrary to God's will for creation, that disengage us from appreciative and responsible engagement with our particular places. These include:

- *Consumerism*, which seeks fulfillment in the endless and futile pursuit, possession, and enjoyment of consumer "goods," leading instead to spiritual emptiness, social injustice, and environmental degradation.
- *Dehumanization*, the reduction of human beings to things to be used, or to subhuman "aliens" and "enemies" to be repelled or destroyed.
- *Disregard for creation*, which ignores the complexity, integrity, and intrinsic value of our fellow creatures, reducing them to raw materials for our products and projects.
- The *quest for personal and collective security* by obtaining power over other persons and groups, whether by overt violence or threat thereof, or by withholding the resources and respect that they need to be full participants in and beneficiaries of the community.

For the sake of God's creation, we must be released from the ethos and worldview of which values and practices such as these are a part.

We are freed *for* the world in the sense that the point of our liberation is to enable us to live out our vocation to be neighbors to others (Luke 10:27-37) as participants in community and as creatures within creation. As Luther said, "A Christian is perfectly free lord of all, subject to none. A Christian is a perfectly dutiful servant of all, subject to all."[2] Furthermore, the gospel is the good news of the restoration of humanity in Christ, as Terence Fretheim writes: "*The objective of God's work in redemption is to free people to be what they were created to be*. It is a deliverance not from the world, but to true life in the world."[3] In affirming our baptism, we commit ourselves to "bearing God's creative and redeeming word to all the world."[4] We are not just to proclaim the good news of the gospel, we are to *be* good news rather than "bad news." Our restoration in Christ includes restoration to our original vocation, that is, to be servers and keepers of creation. Good news indeed—for people and for the rest of creation!

So, how does a church building—especially the sanctuary—express the "freedom from/freedom for" dialectic of Christian faith in relation to its surroundings? The church building usually announces the congregation's aspiration to freedom from the world by looking *like* a church. Traditional forms and symbols—steeple, cross, stained-glass windows, and so on—may be used to signal that a building is a church, whether it is a soaring cathedral or a simple cinder-block structure that would look like a warehouse without such markers. Even more contemporary churches that try to avoid the clichés of church architecture try to express something of the same quality of difference and transcendence.

When a congregation uses and manages its property and building in a way that is responsive and responsible to the wider community, it physically embodies in its particular place the "freedom for" side of the dialectic. The gardens, prairie plantings, rainwater irrigation system, solar panels, and so forth at churches like MCC are not only aesthetic or utilitarian but also express by their symbolic associations the belief that the whole creation is God's, and that its care and keeping are a proper concern of Christian communities. When a church opens its building to a food pantry, meal site, day care, homeless shelter, or other community service, it concretely expresses the gracious hospitality that is the proper Christian response to God's all-embracing grace.

Gathering Time

The sanctified time in which the congregation regularly gathers for worship and study is the Sabbath. Of course, members of the congregation may meet for worship and study at other times of the week as well, but the Sunday morning assembly remains the paradigm for "church time." Families or individuals may also "keep the Sabbath" not only by going to church, but also by setting aside other special times for quiet prayer and reflection, whether on Sunday or during the week.

Whenever and however it is done, Sabbath observance can be seen as a process of three movements or acts:

1. *Disengaging*: Setting aside what distracts or diverts us from growing in discipleship—the busyness of household and workplace; the fog of superficial entertainment; the false values, practices, and perceptions of the dominant culture; the comfortable cocoon of preoccupation with self, and so on: "Be still, and know that I am God" (Ps. 46:10).

2. *Discerning*: Once we have created a mental breathing space by setting aside the clutter of daily life, we can focus on what is of ultimate importance. Not only through prayer, Bible study, and meditation, but also by attending to God's grace and justice in our particular contexts: delighting in the goodness and wonder of creation; being fully present to other persons as images and children of God; and listening to and lifting up the litany of the world's suffering.

3. *Reengaging*: Immersing ourselves again in the flow of daily life, but with a refreshed perspective, informed by what we have discerned in our Sabbath time, both as a deeper appreciation for God's sustaining and renewing presence in our lives, and as a critical judgment on all that blocks and undermines the wholeness and holiness that God wills for all creation.

This dialectic of disengagement/reengagement parallels in a temporal process the dialectics of freed from/freed for (in personal identity) and different/related (in geographical space). The in-between moment of discernment is, in a sense, the moment of formation and cultivation in worship and education. Here again we find another dialectic: that of creation and Scripture. How does Christian discernment hold these together?

Gathered around the Word in the Midst of Creation

When we gather in congregations, Lutherans are focused on the Word—the Word proclaimed in preaching; the Word witnessed in Scripture; the Word made visible in the sacraments; and above all, the Word Incarnate in Jesus Christ. We less often attend to the creation within which we gather, though the scriptural Word tells us that "by the word of the Lord the heavens were made" (Ps. 33:6a). In order to be adequate to both our times and teachings, Christian formation must correct that oversight.

Lutherans have a history of connecting God's Word to earthly elements in the sacraments. Luther stresses in his *Small Catechism* that baptism is water used according to God's command and connected with God's Word. He explains the Word of God is with, in, and among the water and faith that trusts this Word of God in water.[5]

While the Word-element connection is embedded in our understanding of sacramental theology, the Word-element connection in Christian education and worship is weak. Yet, strong and numerous connections exist between words of Scripture and creation. As Fretheim writes, "These hymnic materials are voiced by both human beings and nonhuman creatures; they participate in a mutuality of the praise of God and their praises are interdependent."[6]

There are good reasons to illuminate and incorporate the Word-creation connection into the education ministry and congregation's worship life. First, it helps us to avoid the extremes of desacralization of creation and of pantheism. Second, the biblical notion that creation is valued in its own right in relation to God challenges the anthropocentric understanding that the sole reason for creation's existence is to support and sustain human life only. God loves both humans and nonhumans! Third, we come to see that creation is a seamless web that intimately includes the Creator and there is an interdependent relationship between God, humanity, and creation. Fourth, just as we are better able to praise God when surrounded by a singing community, nature's praise of God broadens our awareness and appreciation of God's praiseworthiness. All of these considerations forge an ecological identity that biblical theology as well as environmental awareness undergird, and thus keep us connected to our place.

As already noted, congregational members are not only gathered into a particular place, they are gathered as families and individuals from the places where they carry out the activities of their daily lives. As God's dispersed people in the world before and after worship, they are encouraged to cultivate their spiritual life outside of Sunday worship. For example, MCC members are encouraged to commit themselves to a set of faith practices that include: "pray daily, worship regularly, study God's Word, respond as stewards, serve at MCC and beyond, cultivate spiritual friendship."

"The Bible should be carried in one hand and the newspaper in the other hand," as Karl Barth is supposed to have said. Another, less obvious connection is that the Scripture and newspapers are printed on the same material, paper. Paper is derived from trees. Scripture's account of salvation history and the daily news are not only set within a place, they are also dependent upon the materials from a place to communicate with the reader. The Bible should be read, studied, and contemplated, not only in relation to history and current events, but also in relation to the wider creation.

To explore the relationship between God's Word and creation, try reading the Bible outdoors. After all, the Bible emerged from a premodern culture that was much closer to the land than are we. Consider the wealth of imagery from the natural world and agricultural life that we find in the prophets, psalms, wisdom literature, and especially Jesus' parables: the sower and the seed (Mark 4:3); the wheat and the tares (Matt. 13:24); the grain of mustard seed (Matt. 13:31); the rich man and his barns (Luke 12:16); the fig tree (Luke 13:6); the vineyard (Luke 20:9).

Reading the Bible outdoors, individually or in small groups, gives us a new way of seeing and interpreting the language of the fields, lakes and wetlands, prairie and desert, trees, forests, bushes and flowers, human and nonhuman communities, the whole material world. It also gives us a new appreciation for the pervasive importance of nature in Scripture. When the Bible is read outdoors it becomes a field guide in praising God.

Word and Creation in Worship and Education

Trees and gardens are two examples of ways that particular, concrete elements of the congregation's environment can be incorporated into its education ministry and worship life.

Trees: The Death of an Oak

The Bur Oak Task Force at MCC was formed in response to the diagnosis that the church's stately, 175-year-old bur oak, cherished by many and carefully attended to through the years, was dying. As the saying goes, "You can't judge a tree by its bark." Sturdy limbs, green leaves, and an abundant annual crop of acorns gave the appearance of good health. However, a large cavity in the trunk and the opinion of three independent arborists prompted us to make plans to commemorate the tree before its felling, in which the entire congregation took part.

A four-week education series became an occasion for participants to contemplate the relationship between trees and sense of place, and to explore biblical references to trees. The Bible's story of salvation history begins and ends with references to symbolic trees. We find the tree of life and the tree of the knowledge of good and evil in the garden of Eden (Gen. 2:9). In Revelation we find the tree of life again in the final eschatological vision of the New Jerusalem (Rev. 22:2): "its leaves are for the healing of the nations, and there will no longer be any curse." Theologian Barbara Rossing contends that the tree of life is one of the most powerful images in Revelation:

> Look up into the trees' branches and see the succulent fruit growing all year long. Can we eat this fruit? Can we touch? These are important questions, because in the Genesis story of creation God specifically told Adam and Eve that the fruit from this tree of life was forbidden. Revelation lifts the Genesis prohibition. The promise to the church in Ephesus is that God's people can now eat of the fruit of the tree of life, a promise of life even better than the Garden of Eden: "To the one who conquers I will give to eat of the fruit of the tree of life that is in the paradise of my God" (Revelation 2:7).[7]

Between Genesis and Revelation is the tree of salvation, the cross, which is the ultimate ground of both curse and blessing, judgment and healing. Paul (Gal. 3:13) speaks of the curse on the sin-bearing Savior who hung on the tree, a theme picked up again by Peter (1 Pet. 2:24). These draw upon the Old Testament tradition that an executed person who is hung on a tree is under God's curse (Deut. 21:23). The cursing of Christ brought about both the destruction of death and the renewal of life and immortality through the gospel; all this came through the tree. As the traditional eucharistic preface for Passion Week says, Christ "on the tree of the cross gave salvation to all, that where death began, there life might be restored and that he who by a tree once overcame, might by a tree be overcome . . ."[8]

A professional storyteller and MCC member told biblical tree stories and coached us in the art of recalling and telling personal tree stories. The pictures and written commentary in R. Bruce Allison's *Every Root an Anchor: Wisconsin's Famous and Historic Trees* heightened our appreciation of all the surprising ways that trees function in the landscapes of our lives. Allison writes, "These tree stories are part of the social history of the state and the personal and emotional history of people. Affection for trees has influenced our behavior. Trees have served as anchors for time-honored family and community customs, as manifestations of ideals and as reminder of significant events."[9]

Children combed the grass under the tree like squirrels and filled grocery bags with acorns. One evening seventh- and eighth-grade confirmation students spread a large tarp on the education unit floor, separated good acorns from bad acorns, cracked the shells open, and picked out small chunks of pulp. A mother and daughter found a Native American recipe for acorn bread, which, placed on the altar became the bread of life at Sunday worship, nourishing our spiritual hunger. The taste of acorn reminded us of all the ways a single tree nourishes human and nonhuman life: by sheltering birds, squirrels, and bugs, and by inviting people to repose under the shade of its outstretched limbs.

The bur oak became the focus of MCC's stewardship emphasis that year. A thematic statement for the fall connected trees and stewardship:

> In drawing energy and nutrients from the sun, soil, air and rain, a tree not only sustains its own life, but it gives life to other creatures—the birds that nest in it, the insects that live in its bark and feed on its leaves, the animals that eat its seeds or fruit. Just so, our gifts to our congregation not only sustains the life of this worshiping community, but are spread abroad to our neighbors, our community and the creation.

Want to learn about stewardship? Study the life of a tree. Stewardship begins by tending to the individual roots of members and the congregation's taproot. Pastors and congregational leaders are responsible for protecting, preserving, nurturing our individual and corporate roots. We work the soil around the tree so the roots can receive nourishment. The soil is being worked whenever we gather for worship, whenever God's Word of life and love is proclaimed, whenever two or three come together in Jesus' name. The soil of our lives and of the congregation's life is being worked with the hope that the root system will move deeper—deeper into the earth, deeper toward truthfulness, deeper toward living water, deeper toward the Source of Life, deeper toward God.

Sometimes we wonder if tending to the soil makes any difference. Nevertheless, we resist the urge to dig a hole to see how the roots are doing. Roots are to remain hidden. This is God's domain and we trust God's Spirit to extend the roots toward deepness. Yet leaves and roots are not directly connected, but only by the tree's trunk and branches. To quote a prayer by biblical scholar Walter Brueggemann: "This is how it is when we praise you. We join the angels in praise, and we keep our feet in time and place. . . . awed to heaven, rooted in earth. We are daily stretched between communion with you and our bodied lives, spent but alive, summoned and cherished but stretched between."[10] Awed to heaven and rooted to earth, we are stretched by the trunk, with its lifeless bark protecting the invisible flow of Jesus' life between deep roots, clapping leaves (see Isa. 55:12), and generous hearts.

Gardens

> Gardens are spiritually restorative because they mirror, provided they have not gone to Apollonian extremes, the harmony and mutual beneficence that ought to characterize our life within creation. They help us to see what is proper, what is fitting, and what is beautiful. They introduce us to the rhythms of birth, growth, decay, and death and help us see these rhythms as good and not as something to be feared or detested. Is it any wonder, then, that we should often choose for our final resting place sites that resemble gardens?[11]

Part of MCC's property has long been used for community gardens. In the early 1970s, the farmer who had donated the land plowed an area behind the church that was divided into twenty-eight 30-by-40-foot garden plots. An article in a United Church of Christ magazine in 1973 told how praying mantises and ladybugs were used in the MCC "mini-farms" for natural pest control. The article also described the bountiful harvest from the gardens—including "corn, tomatoes, beans, carrots, beets, peas, cucumbers, cabbage, melons, peppers, lettuce, swiss chard"—some of which the women of the church canned or froze.[12] The community gardens remain, and another part of the church's property has since been turned into vegetable gardens, for a project that will be described in chapter 4.

Personal experience tells us that gardens are meaningful places. Homeowners plant gardens to beautify their property. Individuals and groups gather in gardens in rural areas, towns, and cities to plant and tend gardens for the benefit of a few family members and friends or entire community. Newlyweds or prom-goers remember their special occasions by posing for pictures in a garden.

The theme of gardens and gardening therefore provides rich possibilities for linking an experience of place shared by many congregational members—whether their own home gardens or the church's gardens—and Scripture. Biblical references from the prophets speak of gardens as places of restoration following periods of scarcity or exile: "For the Lord will comfort Zion; he will comfort all her waste places, and will make her wilderness like Eden, her desert like the garden of the LORD; joy and gladness will be found in her, thanksgiving and the voice of song" (Isa. 51:3; see also Isa. 58:11; Jer. 31:12; Ezek. 36:35; Hos. 14:7; Mic. 7:14). The Easter text from John's Gospel, where Mary Magdalene encounters the resurrected Jesus outside the tomb (20:1-18), offers an easily overlooked opportunity for connecting the core of Christian faith to a common experience of place, an ethic and spirituality of care and nurture, and the recovery of our human vocation to "serve and keep" the earth.

Jesus the Master Gardener

The Gospel Passion narratives receive concentrated attention in a congregation's liturgical life during Holy Week. Each scene, beginning with Jesus' entry into Jerusalem and culminating with Jesus' resurrection from the dead, lends credibility to the narrative's theological underpinnings. Jesus' final destination is Jerusalem because of the religious and political symbolism that is deeply embedded there. After Jesus' death Joseph of Arimathea asks Pilate to allow him to take Jesus' body and lay it to rest in an empty tomb in a nearby garden. Is the place where Jesus' body was placed any more or less significant than his presence in the Temple, or before Pilate, or on Golgotha?

According to John's Gospel Mary Magdalene mistakes the Risen Christ for the gardener. We are quick to excuse Mary for this oversight and move on to celebrate Jesus' true identity as the crucified and risen Savior. But what if we allow Jesus as the Gardener and Risen One to linger as a metaphor for God's restoration of creation and reconciliation with humanity? The garden near Golgotha is a contrast to Eden, the first garden, even as Christ the "second Adam" is in contrast to the "first Adam" (1 Cor. 15:22, 45). Adam and Eve failed to trust God and were ordered to leave the garden. Jesus as the resurrected Gardener restores and redeems humanity's place in the garden.

In John's Gospel we are invited to ponder who Jesus is through a series of "I Am" sayings: "I am the bread of life"; "I am the vine and you are the branches"; "I am the good shepherd." Imagine Jesus saying, "I am the master gardener." This Master Gardener, through the Holy

Spirit, is present as the Risen One and provides for our nurture. He tills and keeps our souls, quenches our spiritual thirst with living water. He gently pulls weeds and cultivates, waters, and enriches our souls releasing deep joy and gratitude. He animates our lives by deepening our roots in faith and bringing forth fruit to the glory of God.

Granted, such metaphorical language has limitations; nevertheless, Jesus as the Master Gardener is an animating metaphor in MCC's preaching and teaching ministry. Even if Jesus never placed a seed in soil, pulled a weed, or picked a vegetable he was born and raised and carried out his ministry in an agrarian setting and repeatedly drew material for teaching and parables from it. Even though North Americans are increasingly disconnected from agrarian life—not only from materials of nature but also from the materials of Jesus' parables—we nevertheless can imagine ourselves back into agrarian settings by placing ourselves physically in gardens where our five senses are engaged as well. Gardening greatly reduces the gap between the ancient agrarian life and our nonagrarian life. The biblical references about planting, uprooting, gleaning and harvesting, casting seed on different types of soil, separating wheat and tares, bearing good fruit, walking on paths, pruning branches on a vine, and so forth, become real rather than imagined. Although Jesus does not command us to plant and care for gardens, gardening, by its materiality, is sacramental because it reveals God's grace in creation.

Gardens are places where the bonds between gardener and God, fellow gardeners, and nonhuman life is nourished and strengthened. The garden is as much a place for teaching Bible stories as a church classroom. The MCC youth education committee decided in 2008 to forego the annual week of Vacation Bible School and instead piloted a garden ministry for elementary-age children. The theme, "Nurturing Soil and Soul: MCC Kids in the Garden," was lifted up for thirteen summer Sundays. A core group of parents gardened with the children for an hour after worship. Every Sunday included a biblical theme related to gardening. First fruits of the harvest were placed upon the altar for worship. Vegetables were gleaned and donated to a food pantry. Produce was shared with all MCC members. Every gathering of gardeners concluded with a snack, usually freshly picked vegetables from the garden. MCC member Tom Hind composed a theme song that was sung every week. A "Seeds for Faith" packet was sent home with children every week to reinforce each week's lesson, including growing points (the Bible passage and devotional writing), seeds for thought (an activity linking the lesson and environment), and "soul water" (a weekly prayer).

The children and adult gardeners had a delightful time working (playing?) together in the garden. Harvesting an abundant, varied crop of vegetables was a joyous time. No tests were administered to determine the growth of each child's biblical and ecological literacy, but one of the adults shared this revealing story: "You can't lie to the earth," ten-year-old Ruth stated emphatically one Sunday as she looked at a photo she had taken of a habanero pepper plant. "The earth knows when you are lying," Ruth continued, "I might tell you I watered, but the plants know I didn't. And they will tell that I didn't."

A woman from the neighborhood was looking for a congregation to join. She was by herself the first Sunday she joined the congregation for worship. The next Sunday she returned with her two young sons in tow and brought them out to garden after worship. After a time of harvesting squash, beans, Swiss chard, beets, and basil, six-year-old Eagan shouted out to his mom, "I'm going to like this church!"

Gathering Place, Gathering Time, Gathered People

These examples illustrate how Christian formation can take place at the intersection of time, place, and identity in the congregation's gathering for worship and instruction. Congregants bring their own memories and stories of their encounters with creation—in these cases, of trees and gardens—into the place of worship. The place of worship itself provides opportunities for awareness, appreciation, and care for a part of creation as members work in the gardens, share the produce, inspect and worry about the health of the bur oak, or even just see the plants and the tree (or its absence) on their way to and from worship. Sabbath time provides the mental space and detachment from daily concerns to allow reflection and conversation that adds new meaning to these "ordinary" and "mundane" experiences by setting them within the context of the biblical story of creation and redemption.

Through gathering in this place and in this time, the congregants receive new points of orientation, new maps and metaphors for interpreting their own identity. They can see themselves as stewards on the earth, whose possessions are not their own but, rather, gifts that, through their church, can sustain others. They are recipients of the Master Gardener's tender nurturing, but also called upon to "bear fruit that befits repentance." They are invited to live not by "worldly" standards of self-seeking consumerism or security through violence, but by biblical standards of self-giving, responsibility, and care.

Questions for Reflection and Discussion

1. In what ways have you experienced being freed from the world for the world? What hinders or helps such freedom?

2. In what ways has the Word-creation connection been incorporated into your congregation's education ministry and worship life?

3. How do you feel about the metaphor of Jesus as Gardener compared to other metaphors used to describe the resurrected Christ?

4. Are there trees and gardens that have been important to your life? Have they affected your spiritual understanding?

4

A Countercultural Community of Celebration and Care

> God—man—nature! These three are meant for each other, and restlessness will stalk our hearts and ambiguity our world until their cleavage is redeemed.
>
> —Joseph Sittler[1]

Peter once gave a presentation on "Congregations and the Gift of Place" to an academic audience in southern Illinois, using slides and stories about the activities of Madison Christian Community. During the discussion that followed, an environmental philosopher asked a penetrating question: Do the members of the congregation see their actions as profoundly countercultural—subverting the dominant cultural values that regard the natural landscape merely as private property or as a resource that the owner can develop or dispose of without regard for social or environmental consequences? Or are they merely fashionably "green" feel-good activities that raise no deeper questions about cultural values or public policies?

This question cannot easily be answered with much confidence or precision. When it was later posed to a MCC adult forum group, some cited several youth from the congregation who had gone into environmental professions as evidence that MCC's place-based practices did contribute to forming an ecological conscience in its members. But perhaps the most we can say at present is that it is our hunch and hope that the sort of intentional cultivation of values and awareness described in chapter 3 will ultimately lead to a critical perspective on the wider society's values and practices, and to individual and group action to change those values and practices for the better.

How might this happen? How does an understanding of the mission of the church informed by a "sense of place" work itself out in the congregation's relationship to its surrounding community? What forms of service to the people and places outside the edges of its property might a congregation's ministry take? Does the congregation simply model an alternative way of being "in place" or can it also influence the way that the persons and institutions in the community and wider culture understand and interact with their places?

Christian Responsibility as Stewardship

A congregation's concern for its place can be undermined by attitudes and beliefs that tend to minimize the religious significance of everyday material and social reality. Often Christian hope is understood to be a yearning for an escape from this world, whether by retreating into a detached piety of inner peace and holiness or by attaining a heavenly home after death. In that case, the Christian has little stake, religiously speaking, in the future of the world: whether on a large scale, as the fate of the earth; or small, as the flourishing or decay of the local community. Of course, inner peace and eternal life are *part* of the meaning of Christian hope, and people do care about their communities and the environment even if they don't relate that caring to their spiritual life or the church's mission. But the hope of which Scripture speaks is expressed in earthy, world-embracing imagery of healing and harmony for and with all creation (for example, Isa. 43:19-21 and Rev. 21:1—22:6). Viewed within this biblical frame, the congregation's mission to its community and the wider world is one of witness and service to God's coming *shalom*—to healthy and peaceful relationships between God, people, and the earth. A congregation that deals with its own small patch of creation and participates in its community out of such an understanding of mission directly challenges unjust and destructive values and practices in its surrounding culture.

One concept that has been frequently used to express Christians' responsible participation in worldly affairs is "stewardship." The range of understandings about stewardship is so broad that it often gets reduced to simplistic slogans. "Stewardship is everything that comes after saying, 'I believe'"; "Stewardship is how we respond to all that God has given and entrusted to us"; "Stewardship is using our time, talents, and treasures in service to the community and to the glory of God." A more adequate understanding of stewardship, one that will enable us more properly to appreciate and take responsibility for God's gift of the places in which we find ourselves, requires that we more fully include the rest of creation as humanity's partner, companion, and co-worker in between God's beginning and end.

"The earth is the LORD's and all that is in it, the world, and those who live in it" (Ps. 24:1). Stewardship begins with God. As Supreme Giver (James 1:17), God fills the world with abundance. The earth and its fullness remain God's and we are the recipients of God's gifts. God's people recognize that all good things are gifts from God and, when we respond by using those gifts responsibly, we practice stewardship.

Stewardship also ends—finds its goal and purpose—in God. God does not give up ownership of the world. The standard for what counts as responsible stewardship is our best understanding of what God intends, wills, and does in the world. The Greek word we translate as stewardship is *oikonomia*—the management of the household. The Greek word for home or household is *oikos,* which is the root of our words *ecology* (the orderly relationship of living things to their homes and to their fellow inhabitants), *economy* (the management of the household and its resources), and *ecumenical* (the inhabited world). We have noted how creation is God's establishing a home for life—a cosmic household, as it were. God's stewardship—God's "economy" or plan for the household of the entire world—is summed up in the proposition that God wills to reconcile the world to Godself in Christ (2 Cor. 5:19; Col. 1:20). God intends creation to be a whole, healthy community in communion with God's self. Stewardship ends in God.

So, God created and is creating, God redeemed and is redeeming, and God sanctifies and continues to set the redeemed apart as those who live within the plan and carry out God's mission. As God's people and God's stewards, we participate in God's creating, redeeming, and sanctifying activity. God's people share in God's mission for the world. God's people know God's will toward the world and proclaim the gospel through words and actions. "Let your light shine before others," Jesus counsels, "so that they may see your good works and give glory to your Father in heaven" (Matt. 5:16).

Indeed, "Stewardship begins and ends with God." The question, "What comes between God's beginning and end?" begs to be answered. More often than not, the focus is solely on humanity's role between God's beginning and end, with the rest of creation at best playing a secondary role as a supporting platform or raw material for human projects and activity. This understanding suggests that God hands the keys to creation over to humanity. The natural world is open and available to human beings for exploitation and manipulation without limit or restraint.

Humans as imago mundi et dei

Lutheran theology provides a lens through which to look at our relationship to God and to creation: the lens of *simul*s. *Simul*, Latin for "at the same time," is the root of the English word *simultaneously*. *Simul*s do not allow us to divide things dualistically into mutually exclusive camps of either/or, but embrace both/and.

> Lutheran theology understands that God's revelation is simultaneously hidden and revealed; God's activity occurs simultaneously through the work of the left hand and right hand; Christ is simultaneously human and divine; the saving activity of God is simultaneously through law and gospel; the Christian is simultaneously a saint and sinner; the sacrament of bread and wine is simultaneously the body and blood; the kingdom of God is simultaneously present here and now and not yet.[2]

We propose to add one more *simul* to the Lutheran repertoire, following a suggestion by Daniel Deffenbaugh, religion professor and author: humankind is created simultaneously in the image of the earth and in the image of God: *simul imago mundi et dei*.[3]

Who would argue that humanity as image of God has not received top billing from Christian theologians? Moreover, the way *imago dei* ("image of God") has been interpreted has tended to locate the image of God in human beings' unique capacities for reason, freedom, and/or moral responsibility. Deffenbaugh writes,

> The received notion of *imago dei* tended to place human beings outside or above the created order and has to some extent perpetuated the image of the ideal human as an autonomous individual who uses his or her cognitive abilities to discern God's will for creation. The assumption here is that there is some substantive similarity between the Creator and God's image on earth: as God is self-reflective, so are humans.[4]

A different interpretation of *imago dei* and the complementary notion of the *imago mundi* ("image of the earth") is suggested by the story of humanity's creation in Genesis 2:4b—3:24. In contrast to Genesis 1, where God speaks the world into being and sees that it is good, in Genesis 2 we have a Creator who does not act at a distance, but is intimately engaged with creation. The name "Adam," for the first human being, and *adam* as the Hebrew word for humans-in-general, is a play on the Hebrew word *adamah*—earth, tillable soil.[5] Thus, Adam was brought into this world in the same manner as were all nonhuman creatures: created from the earth, of like nature with the rest of creation (see Gen. 2:19). Most striking in this narrative is that, in contrast to the account of humans' creation in Genesis 1:26-27, there is no mention of Adam being created in the image of God. But there is a similarity with the Creator in the task that Adam is later directed to perform: "The LORD God took the man and put him in the garden of Eden to till it and keep it" (Gen. 2:15; see also Gen. 2:8). Just as God nurtures and tends the garden, so must Adam. And in so doing, Adam "images" God. Our similarity to God is found in our caring relationship to the earth rather than in any peculiar human trait or capacity. Deffenbaugh writes, "Ontologically, we are grounded in the earth, with which we share our being. Ethically, our actions should reflect the work of the Creator—we are 'imagers of God.'"[6]

God, Human Beings, and Nature

Therefore, both ethically and ontologically—in terms of what we ought to do, and what kinds of being we are—and both as image of God and image of earth, humans cannot be understood in isolation from the rest of creation. There are strong biblical warrants for the idea that humans and nature belong together between God's beginning and end. In Genesis 1, the parts of creation are good but creation as a whole—day and night, land and sea, birds, fish, animals and humans—is very good. As we saw in chapter 1, in Genesis 2, both human beings and the garden earth need each other.

In the story of Noah, the fate of human beings and the nonhuman creation are inseparable—whether the infection of violence, destruction by deluge, salvation in the ark, or the promise of a future:

> And God saw that the earth was corrupt; for all flesh had corrupted its ways upon the earth. . . . And all flesh died that moved on the earth, birds, domestic animals, wild animals, all swarming creatures that swarm on the earth, and all human beings. . . . But God remembered Noah and all the wild animals and all the domestic animals that were with him in the ark. . . . Then God said to Noah, "Go out of the ark, you and your wife, and your sons and your sons' wives with you. Bring out with you every living thing that is with you of all flesh—birds and animals and every creeping thing that creeps on the earth—so that they may abound on the earth, and be fruitful and multiply on the earth." (Gen. 6:12; 7:21; 8:1a, 15-17)

That theme is carried through in the prophets, as human sin disrupts the nonhuman creation as well as human society, and God's redemption restores both land and people: "Because there has been no rain on the land the farmers are dismayed; they cover their heads. Even the doe in the field forsakes her newborn fawn because there is no grass. The wild asses stand on the bare heights, they pant for air like jackals; their eyes fail because there is no herbage" (Jer. 14:4b-6). "I am about to do a new thing; now it springs forth, do you not perceive it? I will make a way in the wilderness and rivers in the desert. The wild animals will honor me, the jackals and the ostriches; for I give water in the wilderness, rivers in the desert, to give drink to my chosen people, the people whom I formed for myself so that they might declare my praise" (Isa. 43:19-21).

And in the New Testament: "For the creation waits with eager longing for the revealing of the children of God; for the creation was subjected to futility, not of its own will but by the will of the one who subjected it, in hope that the creation itself will be set free from its bondage to decay and will obtain the freedom of the glory of the children of God" (Rom. 8:19-21).

Because God loves us and nonhuman life, we love one another and nonhuman life. Consequently, we move from a hierarchical to a circular understanding of creation. In a hierarchical view of creation, power, authority, and control flow from top to bottom—from God to humans to nature. Obedience and service flow from bottom to top—from nature to humans to God. A circular or cyclical view recognizes the interdependent relationship between God, humans, and nonhuman life. While God remains sovereign, God shares power and creativity with humans, as we saw in chapter 1, but also with the rest of creation. In Genesis 1, creation is not merely passive: the earth "brought forth" vegetation and living creatures (vv. 11-12, 24); birds and fish and humans continue God's creative work by being fruitful and multiplying (vv. 22, 28).

Creation is not a finished work or following a preordained course like a simple computer program or a player piano. Creation continues and is at least somewhat open ended. According to Terence Fretheim, in the Bible, "Human beings are given responsibility for intracreational development, bringing the world along to its fullest possible potential. The creation is a highly dynamic reality in which the future is open to a number of possibilities and creaturely activity is crucial for the becoming of the creation. Creative capacities have been given to the created ones for the task of continuing creation."[7]

The upshot of all this is to suggest that the congregation's care for its property and service to the community should implement, model, and communicate responsible stewardship as the cultivation of creative community of humans and nature—locally to be sure, but perhaps ultimately also reaching out to the global scale. Only a few examples can be given here. In keeping with what has been one of our key texts—Genesis 2—and guiding metaphors—gardening—we will focus on congregational practices and activities that revolve around the growing and distribution of food. In spite of this relatively narrow focus, we hope these examples will illuminate the particular contributions that congregations can make to fostering a way of life that is more respectful and responsible toward the places in which God has set us as recipients, responders, and communicators of grace.

Garden Ministry

People garden for various reasons. For many people, it is an economic necessity, while for others gardening is an enjoyable hobby. When congregational members commit to gardening together for a season the greatest benefit is not the harvest of vegetables but the cultivation of relationships. Gardening cultivates relationships with the Creator, the soil and the place of the garden, and with other gardeners. Gardeners are more than recreationists, they are *re-creationists.* Deffenbaugh writes, "The garden is one place where people can, over a committed period of time—not just a Sunday afternoon here and there—listen and watch patiently, enter into alliances, perform rituals, give thanks, know intimately the myriad person of their community, and experience a sense of living in place."[8]

The nine thousand-square-foot garden at MCC is a partnership between congregational members and Wexford Ridge, a neighborhood center for grade school youth, that began in 2003. During the summer months children and adults gather two mornings a week to work in the garden. Two children are partnered with an adult and they relate to one another affectionately as "garden buddies." The distance between the neighborhood center and the church is only one mile, but the social, economic, and racial distance is much greater. The congregational demographics mirror the demographics of a highly educated workforce in a university setting, while the demographics of people at Wexford Ridge mirror the challenges of a less educated and underemployed population.

Jesus didn't seem to have great difficulty bridging God's kingdom with people on the margins, but many congregations do. A garden ministry is one way that can bridge the racial, economic, and social barriers that exist between people today. The kinds of distinctions Paul describes—"There is neither Jew nor Greek, there is neither slave nor free, there is neither male nor female; for you are all one in Christ Jesus" (Gal. 3:28)—disappear because of the new identity given through Christ. In the garden these distinctions recede and the joys and challenges of gardening are mutually shared.

Most of the vegetable seed for the garden ministry comes from Seed Savers Exchange in Decorah, Iowa. Seed Savers' mission is to collect and preserve heirloom seeds. The seeds are started indoors, then inmates at a nearby correctional facility tend them under the supervision of a horticultural teacher who believes in restorative justice (the idea that the purpose of the judicial system is to restore the offender to a right relationship with society, rather than simply to inflict punishment). These inmates take a field trip to MCC and devote a day to the garden where the seedlings they have cared for will be transplanted. They help prepare for the gardening season by raking the soil, pounding in stakes, attaching fencing, and filling wheelbarrows of mulch for the garden paths. MCC members welcome the inmates with homemade baked goods and Mt. Meru coffee, a fair exchange coffee grown in Tanzania and sold in Wisconsin as part of a partner synod relationship with the Greater Milwaukee Area Synod of the ELCA. Not only is it much better than the institutional coffee the inmates are used to, the African coffee farmers receive a larger share of the profits from sale of their crop than is typical in the coffee business. The congregation greatly appreciates the inmates' work, and hopes that the inmates feel a measure of pride in making a meaningful contribution to this ministry.

The children benefit from gardening in a myriad of ways. They acquire the knowledge and skills to plant and tend a garden. They learn to cook the vegetables, enjoy sampling the fruits of their labor, and are proud to share their bounty with family and friends. They seem to be developing what Annie Grugel, a lead gardener, calls an "eco-identity": "Eco-identity refers to all the different ways people construe themselves in relationship to the natural world—a nonhuman element—as manifested in personality, values, actions and sense of self."[9]

The gardening experience affects children in poignant and unexpected ways. A Hmong girl who moved from Thailand when she was seven could only speak a few words of English the first time she joined our group, but it was immediately obvious that she knew how to garden. Eileen, our oldest gardener, and the girl became a great team working side by side through the summer. Annie had the kids take pictures in the garden and later met with each child to discuss the picture with him or her. The girl took a beautiful picture of the pepper plants. Annie was confused because the pepper patch was not the responsibility of Eileen and the girl. When asked about it, the girl answered, "The peppers look just like the ones that my grandmother and I grew together when I lived in Thailand. They remind me of her and where I came from."

A couple with two young daughters moved from Lincoln, Nebraska, to Madison two years ago. They had only two weekends to find a home in an unfamiliar community. They were previously members of another denomination but after being invited by a couple of other families in the neighborhood to MCC decided to check things out. One of the reasons they were attracted to the neighborhood was that they noticed the garden while making the rounds with the realtor. They concluded, "This must be a good place to live." The combination of invitations to worship from members and the attractive power of the garden aesthetics is affectionately referred to as "veggie evangelism."

MCC members are involved in the garden ministry in ways other than serving as garden buddies. They are happy to take fresh-picked produce home from worship on Sunday mornings. Middle school and high school youth are invited to serve as mentors to the younger children. Another member shared his gift of music and composed a song for the elementary school kids. Educators and counselors help write and craft a faith-based curriculum that nurtures the souls of our children as they nurture the vegetables and flowers rooted in the soil.[10]

Granted, some congregations do not have space even the size of a postage stamp in which to plant a garden, but a congregation does not need nine thousand square feet for a garden ministry. Gardens can be planted on flat rooftops, in clay pots, and on empty and abandoned neighborhood lots. Congregational members with yard space may be willing to turn over the sod and provide a place to garden. If congregational members plant gardens where they live they could plant a row or two of vegetables and donate the produce to a food pantry or soup kitchen. Most often, food pantry items are purchased from the grocery store. When members plant gardens and share produce they are participating more fully in the cycles of creation and more likely to share the fruits of their labor with glad and thankful hearts.

Give Us This Day Our Daily Bread: Food Systems

The petition from the Lord's Prayer, "Give us this day our daily bread," is closely related to this discussion. Bread—or, more generally, food—is a bundle of nutrients that, in the right quantities and combinations, is essential for life. But Jesus reminds us in the first temptation in the wilderness that "One does not live by bread alone, but by every word that comes from the mouth of God" (Matt. 4:4). Jesus also says, "I am the bread of life" (John 6:35). Were we merely material beings, these latter statements would make no sense: life requires material bread, and that's it. Were we merely spiritual beings, the petition would make no sense, for material bread would be unnecessary as well as insufficient ("not by bread *alone*"). Even if our bodies were merely useful vehicles to carry around our spirits, it would be hard to account for Jesus' use of the metaphor, "bread of life"—why would spirits need even symbolic "bread," much less the sacramental bread and wine of Holy Communion?

But our lives do have both spiritual and material dimensions, more closely intertwined than driver and automobile. Our lives are sustained both by "daily bread" and by God's Word, the Bread of Life. Both are gifts of a gracious God, and both contribute to the same end: abundant life for the creature that is both the image of God and the image of the earth. Material bread—food—also is not "merely" material. Not only is it somehow capable of sacramentally bearing God's grace to us, but even in ordinary uses it is enmeshed in a web of significant relationships. We receive our daily bread here, in this place, through a network of transactions among humans and between humans and the earth that may reach around the world. What are the spiritual qualities of those relationships? How ethical are those transactions? What are their impacts on people, the land, and other creatures? As with our use of water and energy (chapter 2), attending to our own place means attending to the hidden, taken-for-granted support systems that connect it to other places, other people.

The Industrial Bread System

Michael Pollan's insightful book, *The Omnivore's Dilemma*, explores the history and underpinnings of three food systems: the industrial, the organic, and the hunter-gatherer.[11] The dominant system is industrial agriculture. This is the way of growing, producing, transporting food to grocery stores, and getting it on the shelves for consumers at the lowest possible price. Oil is the energy used to drive this bread system, as it fuels tractors, makes fertilizers, and transports food long distances. A small number of transnational corporations controls this bread system.

The cost of this bread system to the environment, animals, and production laborers is well documented, but it also has a spiritual cost. Industrial agriculture has turned food, once understood as a gift from God, into a commodity to be purchased. Our relationship with food is transactional. You add vegetables, bread, honey, meat, and milk to your grocery cart and pay for them when you go through the checkout line. It's all quite efficient. But where does God fit into this system? We can track the milk in the cooler back to the cow, nourished by genetically modified seed corn, picked from a cornfield smothered with pesticides that kill everything except the corn. Ultimately the water, sunlight, and soil—and oil—can be traced back as gifts from God. Is this what goes through our minds when we stand before the cooler to pick out a gallon of milk? Do we give thanks to God? Do we consider the cost to the earth or how much the farmer was paid for it? Hardly—we look for the lowest price! And we call this rational consumer behavior in a free-trade, market-driven economy.

The Subsistence Bread System

If industrial agriculture is at one end of the spectrum, the system at the other end is the bread system of subsistence. Andrew, a former MCC member with a background in environmental studies, moved with his family to Sitka, Alaska, several years ago to work with the Sitka Conservancy Society. On a visit back to Madison, he commented that many of the people in Sitka catch fish, hunt deer, dig for clams, and grow a limited variety of garden produce. This bread system is one of subsistence. Few, if any of us, fall into this system. But if you have ever gardened and harvested vegetables, or caught a fish, or shot game, you know that it is a different experience than picking up a few items at the grocery store.

Relatively speaking, the subsistence bread system is more closely linked to God as the giver. We are not suggesting that anyone quit buying groceries at the store and go out and forage for food. At the same time, most of us can make food choices based upon more reasons than buying at the lowest possible cost. We can do our homework and seek more information than the nutritional value and ingredients on the package: How far has this food been transported? Where was it grown or raised? What chemicals were applied to the produce or what was injected into animal? What was the animal fed? We can also take advantage of locally grown food and grass-fed livestock, consider becoming a member of a community-supported farm, and plant a garden. We might think of these actions as spiritual disciplines.

Many MCC members like to shop at the Madison farmer's market, one of the nation's largest and most acclaimed, on Saturday mornings. There they buy yogurt from the people whose picture is on the container, tomatoes from the grower, milk from the dairy farmer. We bump into more members of the congregation at the farmer's market than anywhere else we go, and seeing them in this context reinforces our convictions about notions about place. The food MCC families purchase at the market brings greater delight to mealtime fellowship, thus magnifying our gratitude to God, the giver: "You open your hand, satisfying the desire of every living thing" (Ps. 145:16).

Harvest of Hope

God's gift of place includes opportunities to engage in the ordering of our common life. It is right and necessary for the church to stay out of politics in the sense of partisan party politics, election campaigns, and so on. But politics in the broader sense—the process of making decisions about the distribution and deployment of resources and power within a community, and about the rights and responsibilities of its members—cannot be avoided by Christians who are responsive to God's summons to "seek the welfare of the city where I have sent you into exile, and pray to the LORD on its behalf, for in its welfare you will find your welfare" (Jer. 29:7), to "speak out for those who cannot speak . . . defend the rights of the poor and needy" (Prov. 31:8-9), and to "serve and keep the garden" of the earth (Gen. 2:15).

We all know that too many people do not have enough to eat, or the resources and opportunities to purchase local or organically grown food, or the knowledge to prepare the most nutritious meals with the resources they have. Mention of this fact often turns our minds to distant countries where abject poverty, severe environmental degradation, and malnutrition and starvation hold sway. Yet there is hunger here at home as well. In Wisconsin, one in eleven households is "food insecure"—meaning that they don't have regular, reliable access to enough nutritious food for a healthy, active life.[12]

It is a bitter irony that these conditions are experienced by many of those who grow the food. Over the last several decades, small family farmers in particular have struggled to stay afloat in an economy that makes a priority of supplying cheap food to consumers. The 1980s were the decade of "the farm crisis," when the issue broke into the public consciousness—but it has never really gone away. The vagaries of weather, which have always made farming a chancy enterprise, compound the economic problems. The snow was so deep in the winter of 1986 in southern Wisconsin that farmers could not pick corn with mechanical pickers. MCC members organized a Pick and Glean Project where 150 volunteers helped two farmers pick their corn by hand. Following this effort, the Harvest of Hope fund was established to provide assistance to local farmers experiencing financial crisis. Over the past twenty-one years, $731,000 has been contributed to this fund. Harvest of Hope grants offer hope and help to rekindle families' energies for resolving difficult situations. The fund has helped hundreds of farmers stay in business, has helped dozens retain their electric power, has helped some transition out of farming, and, in a few cases, has prevented depressed farmers from committing suicide.

There are a variety of personal circumstances that contribute to someone's difficulty in obtaining food: mental illness, age, lack of education, disrupted family circumstances, alcohol or other drug addiction, difficulties in reentering society after military service or incarceration. But there is also an ecology of hunger and food insecurity, interconnected conditions and causes that vary in their relative significance from place to place, but are generally involved wherever hunger and food insecurity are problems. They include local economic conditions that cause high unemployment or depress wages; high costs of medical insurance, housing, and energy; "food deserts," where stores or markets with inexpensive, quality food are few and far between; lack of public transportation; and so on. Food pantries, soup kitchens, community gardens, and other services supported by congregations can help meet immediate, short-term needs.

However, addressing root causes requires more. It requires attentiveness to place in the form of a closer examination of the ecology of hunger in a particular community and the social, political, and economic forces underlying it. In order to address seriously these root causes, individuals and congregations may have to move outside their comfort zones—into the unfamiliar and contentious areas of community organizing and public policy advocacy.

* * *

As we saw in chapter 2, thinking of a congregation's place in very local, particular terms does not mean thinking of it as hermetically sealed off from the rest of the world—quite the opposite. Just as water pipes and power lines, water runoff and patterns of atmospheric circulation connect the church's use of water and energy to the surrounding physical environment, the congregation also interacts with the surrounding community and culture through the weekly circulation of its members between sacred and secular space, and through the visible witness of its material presence. The practice of tending a garden in collaboration with others is not only a fashionably "green" thing to do. When practiced with and on behalf of those who are marginalized, vulnerable, and who come from differing socioeconomic situations or ethnic backgrounds, it represents a paradigm for a human way of dwelling on the earth that contrasts starkly with the dominant cultural ethos of individualistic consumerism, ecological exploitation, and social fragmentation.

What ultimately may come of cultivating a countercultural eco-identity in a young child, or of helping an adult to learn what it means to be *imago mundi/imago dei* by getting dirt under her fingernails? We cannot know, any more than we can know the full potential of a seed in the ground: "If you really examined a kernel of grain thoroughly, you would die of wonderment" (Martin Luther).[13]

Questions for Reflection and Discussion

1. How does the notion that humanity is created in the image of God and the earth affect your understanding of what it means to be human?

2. Does the understanding of stewardship presented here challenge your personal understanding? Why or why not?

3. In what ways can you participate in food systems that contribute to the common good of humans and nonhumans?

4. What sorts of service or advocacy activities might your congregation undertake that would enhance your community's quality of life and environmental integrity?

Epilogue

> Go in peace. Serve the Lord. . . . Share the good news. . . . Remember the poor. . . . Christ is with you.
>
> —*Evangelical Lutheran Worship*[1]

With these words, the church gathered in worship becomes the church sent into the surrounding community.

The worship and educational practices of the church prepare the ground for Christian engagement in public life by providing teachings, symbols, and narratives that instill values and beliefs that run counter to many of those that dominate American culture today, such as the pursuit of prosperity through environmental and social exploitation, the quest for security through violence and the threat of violence. Prayers of lamentation and praise, Sabbath keeping as the practice of delight in creation and disengagement from the accelerating treadmill of production and consumption, are, in this sense, profoundly countercultural activities that ground and energize the church's witness to and reengagement with the wider culture.

What can members carry with them as they reenter their places of home and family life, work, shopping, recreation, and civic engagement? The following list briefly summarizes what a congregation can contribute, through teachings and practices grounded in place, to shape habits of mind and heart for a more responsible and sustainable society:

1. *Move* the physical infrastructure and systems on which we depend from the background to the foreground of our awareness, so that we can no longer take them for granted;

2. *Focus* attention on the intangible, but physically and biologically grounded, factors that make for quality of life—such as beauty, community, and contact with nature;

3. *Enable* experiences that foster an individual's "eco-identity" and attachment to and empathy with the natural world;

4. *Provide* opportunities for direct experience of one's personal ability to preserve, restore, or enhance creation;

5. *Cultivate* appreciation for the integrity and independent reality of the natural world as God's creation;

6. *Foster* a social and environmental ethic of responsibility, hospitality, care, and interdependence;

7. *Witness* to the power of the gospel of Christ to sustain persistent and creative engagement with a wounded world, and to motivate opposition to all the forces that would degrade and destroy it.

The congregation's social and environmental ministry and advocacy in and for its community is its witness to the good news of God's love for humanity and the earth, and its participation in God's redemptive activity to heal creation. The congregation's response to the grace of God in Word and Sacrament, nature and culture in its specific location can take many forms.[2] Providing affordable, environmentally responsible housing; promoting community food security and sustainable food systems; ensuring a healthy environment and affordable access to health care for the most vulnerable; supporting ecologically sound community planning and environmental policy are only a few of the ways that a congregation can serve God by serving and witnessing to the community in which God has placed it.

A church that celebrates the whole creation as the theater of God's grace in word, deed, and design; that cultivates an ethos of personal responsibility for the well-being of neighbor and neighborhood; that advocates for a politics of compassion and an economy of care, is profoundly countercultural. Viewed against the backdrop of the current crisis of culture manifest in global injustice and environmental degradation, this ministry and advocacy may seem slight and trivial. Yet by God's grace it may become yeast that leavens the whole lump of dough (Matt. 13:33).

Notes

Chapter 1

1. H. Richard Niebuhr, with Daniel Day Williams and James M. Gustafson, *The Purpose of the Church and Its Ministry: Reflections on the Aims of Theological Education* (New York: Harper & Bros., 1956), 38.

2. "Service of Morning Prayer," in *Evangelical Lutheran Worship* (Minneapolis: Augsburg Fortress, 2006), 304.

Chapter 2

1. *Evangelical Lutheran Worship* (Minneapolis: Augsburg Fortress, 2006), 284, 254.

2. "Propers for Daily Prayer," in *Lutheran Book of Worship* (Minneapolis: Augsburg, 1978), 174.

3. "Holy Baptism," in *ELW,* 229.

4. Ibid., 227.

5. Ibid., 230.

6. Mark Hanson, "Waters of Life," *The Lutheran* 21, no. 2 (February 2008): 54.

7. Kristofer Skrade, *The Lutheran Handbook* (Minneapolis: Augsburg Fortress, 2005), 214.

8. "ENERGY STAR Congregations Award Winners," http://www.energystar.gov/index.cfm?c=sb_success.congregations_winners, accessed May 11, 2008.

9. "This is the Feast," in the "Hymn of Praise" section of the various settings for Holy Communion found in the *Lutheran Book of Worship* (Minneapolis: Augsburg, 1978). Based on Rev. 5:13.

10. Terence E. Fretheim, *God and World in the Old Testament: A Relational Theology of Creation* (Nashville: Abingdon, 2005), 264–65.

11. Ibid., 264.

12. Gerard Manley Hopkins, "God's Grandeur," in *Poems of Gerard Manley Hopkins,* 3d ed. (New York: Oxford University Press, 1948), 70.

13. "The Prairie of the Madison Christian Community," LAK [Lois A. Komai], n.d.

Chapter 3

1. For a classic discussion of "sacred space," see Mircea Eliade, "Sacred Space and Making the World Sacred," in his *The Sacred and the Profane*, trans. Willard Trask (New York: Harcourt, Brace, Jovanovich, 1959), 20–65.

2. Martin Luther, "The Freedom of a Christian," in *Martin Luther: Selections from his Writings*, ed. John Dillenberger (Garden City, N.Y.: Anchor, 1961), 53.

3. Terence E. Fretheim, "The Reclamation of Creation: Redemption and Law in Exodus," *Interpretation* 45 (1991): 359; italics in original.

4. "Holy Baptism," in *Evangelical Lutheran Worship* (Minneapolis: Augsburg Fortress, 2006), 231.

5. Kristofer Skrade, *The Lutheran Handbook* (Minneapolis: Augsburg Fortress, 2005), 223.

6. Terence E. Fretheim, *God and World in the Old Testament: A Relational Theology of Creation* (Nashville: Abingdon, 2005), 249.

7. Barbara Rossing, *The Rapture Exposed: The Message of Hope in the Book of Revelation* (Boulder: Westview, 2004), 154.

8. *Lutheran Book of Worship, Minister's Edition* (Minneapolis: Augsburg, 1978), 285.

9. R. Bruce Allison, *Every Root an Anchor: Wisconsin's Famous and Historic Trees*, 2d ed. (Madison: Wisconsin Historical Society, 2005), xi.

10. Walter Brueggemann, *Awed to Heaven, Rooted in Earth: Prayers of Walter Brueggemann*, ed. Edwin Searcy (Minneapolis: Fortress Press, 2003), 85.

11. Norman Wirzba, *The Paradise of God: Renewing Religion in an Ecological Age* (New York: Oxford University Press, 2003), 118.

12. *UCC Life*, January 1973, n.p.

Chapter 4

1. Joseph Sittler, "A Theology for Earth" in *Evocations of Grace*, ed. Steve Bouma-Prediger and Peter Bakken (Grand Rapids: Eerdmans, 2000), 30.

2. Richard H. Bliese and Craig Van Gelder, eds, *The Evangelizing Church: A Lutheran Contribution* (Minneapolis: Augsburg Fortress, 2005), 101.

3. Daniel Deffenbaugh, *Learning the Language of the Fields: Tilling and Keeping as Christian Vocation* (Cambridge: Cowley, 2006), 105–15.

4. Ibid., 107. See also Douglas John Hall, *Imaging God: Dominion as Stewardship* (Grand Rapids: Eerdmans, 1986), for a similar analysis of what it means for humans to be images of God.

5. Theodore Hiebert, *The Yahwist's Landscape: Nature and Religion in Early Israel* (New York: Oxford University Press, 1996), 34–36.

6. Deffenbaugh, *Learning the Language,* 107. "Ontologically" refers to the general characteristics or nature of that which exists.

7. Terence E. Fretheim, *God and World in the Old Testament: A Relational Theology of Creation* (Nashville: Abingdon, 2005), 277.

8. Deffenbaugh, *Learning the Language,* 59.

9. Annie Grugel, "Voices from the Garden: Ecological Narratives of Ideological Becoming," unpublished paper, 2008.

10. Journalist Debra Illingworth Greene wrote an article about the ministry, "Garden Ministry Grows More Than Vegetables," *The Lutheran* 21, no. 5 (May 2008): 22–24.

11. Michael Pollan, *The Omnivore's Dilemma: A Natural History of Four Meals* (New York: Penguin, 2006), 7.

12. Mark Nord, Margaret Andrews, and Steven Carlson, *Household Food Security in the United States, 2006,* United States Department of Agriculture Economic Research Report No. (ERR-49), November 2007, 2–4, 55.

13. Quoted in Heinrich Bornkamm, *Luther's World of Thought,* trans. Martin H. Bertram (St. Louis: Concordia, 1958), 184.

Epilogue

1. Alternative dismissals from *Evangelical Lutheran Worship* (Minneapolis: Augsburg Fortress, 2006); see, for example, p. 115.

2. For more extended reflections on Christian environmental responsibility as a gracious response to God's grace in creation, see Joseph Sittler, "A Theology for Earth" in *Evocations of Grace,* ed. Steve Bouma-Brediger and Peter Bakken (Grand Rapids: Eerdmans, 2000) esp. 179–90.

For Further Reading

Beatley, Timothy. *Native to Nowhere: Sustaining Home and Community in a Global Age*. Washington, D.C.: Island, 2004.

Brown, William P. *The Ethos of the Cosmos: The Genesis of Moral Imagination in the Bible*. Grand Rapids: Eerdmans, 1999.

Brueggemann, Walter. *The Land: Place as Gift, Promise, and Challenge in Biblical Faith*. 2d ed. Minneapolis: Fortress Press, 2002.

Christensen, Laird, and Hal Crimmel, eds. *Teaching about Place: Learning from the Land*. Reno: University of Nevada Press, 2008.

Inge, John. *A Christian Theology of Place*. Aldershot, Hampshire, U.K.: Ashgate, 2005.

Lathrop, Gordon W. *Holy Ground: A Liturgical Cosmology*. Minneapolis: Fortress Press, 2003.

Rasmussen, Larry L. *Earth Community, Earth Ethics*. Maryknoll, N.Y.: Orbis, 1996.

Santmire, H. Paul. *Nature Reborn: The Ecological and Cosmic Promise of Christian Theology*. Minneapolis: Fortress Press, 2000.

Printed in the United States
143271LV00007BA/28/P

9 780806 680125